Antiques at a Glance

SILVER

Antiques at a Glance

SILVER

James Mackay

PRC

First published 2002 by
PRC Publishing Ltd,
64 Brewery Road, London N7 9NT

A member of **Chrysalis** Books plc

This edition published 2002
Distributed in the U.S. and Canada by:
Sterling Publishing Co., Inc.
387 Park Avenue South
New York, NY 10016

ISBN 1 85648 647 8

Printed and bound in China

All the images were kindly supplied by © Christie's
Images Ltd 2002.

Contents

Introduction

Humanity is perhaps not unique in the habit of storing up objects for their own sake, but is the only animal capable of translating material possessions into other values and assessing their worth in terms of hard cash.

According to *The Encyclopaedia Britannica* "antique" means "old" but also carries connotations of esthetic, historic, or financial value. Formerly the term was applied to the remains of the classical cultures of Greece and Rome, which are now more specifically labeled as "antiquities," but gradually "decorative arts, courtly, bourgeois and peasant, of all past eras came to be considered antique."

This definition is somewhat vague, though it hints that mere age alone is not sufficient to make an object worthy of the appellation "antique." *The Oxford English Dictionary* is even more vague in its definition: "Having existed since olden times; of a good age, venerable, old-fashioned, antiquated such as is no longer extant; out of date, behind the times, stale; of, belonging to, or after the manner of any ancient time; a relic of ancient art, of bygone days."

The legal definition of an antique also varied considerably from one country to another. The United Kingdom Customs and Excise Tariff Act of 1930 specified that objects manufactured before 1830 (i.e. a hundred years old or more) would be regarded as antique and therefore exempt from payment of duty on import. The United States Tariff Act of 1930 exempted from duty "Artistic antiquities, collections in illustration of the progress of the arts, objects of art of educational value or ornamental character... which shall have been produced prior to the year 1830." Across the border in Canada, however, their Customs Tariff Act of 1948 defined as antiquities "all objects of educational value and museum interest, if produced prior to 1st January 1847."

Legal definitions, originally designed to cover material a century old, became fixed in such a way as to exclude anything produced after the Regency period. It was often stated that the main reason for adhering to the year 1830 was the fact that craftsmanship deteriorated after that date. For this reason bodies, such as the British Antique Dealers' Association, clung to 1830 as the chronological criterion in defining an antique.

As time passed, however, this inflexible ruling seemed more and more untenable from a purely legal viewpoint, and for the purpose of the avoidance of the payment of import duty the date criterion was subsequently modified in certain countries. The United Kingdom Customs and Excise Tariff Act of 1959, for example, outlined that duty would not be payable on the import of objects, "if manufactured or produced as a whole, and in the form as imported, more than a hundred years before the date of import." More recently, the United States customs adopted a straightforward hundred-year rule, and with the advent of Value Added Tax and similar imposts in other countries, the hundred-year rule is now widely observed.

In periods of economic uncertainty interest in collectable objects tends to increase at the expense of more traditional forms of investment. What used to be the principal motive in collecting —a need to identify with the past—has tended to yield to a need for the form of security that the possession of tangible objects brings when money itself is diminishing in worth and true meaning. It becomes less important to the collector to amass objects of great antiquity, especially since the supply of antiques has become scarcer due to worldwide demand, and leads the collector to turn inevitably to more recent products. For those reasons, many dealers in the 1970s

RIGHT: An English George II basket by Phillips Garden of London dating from 1752.

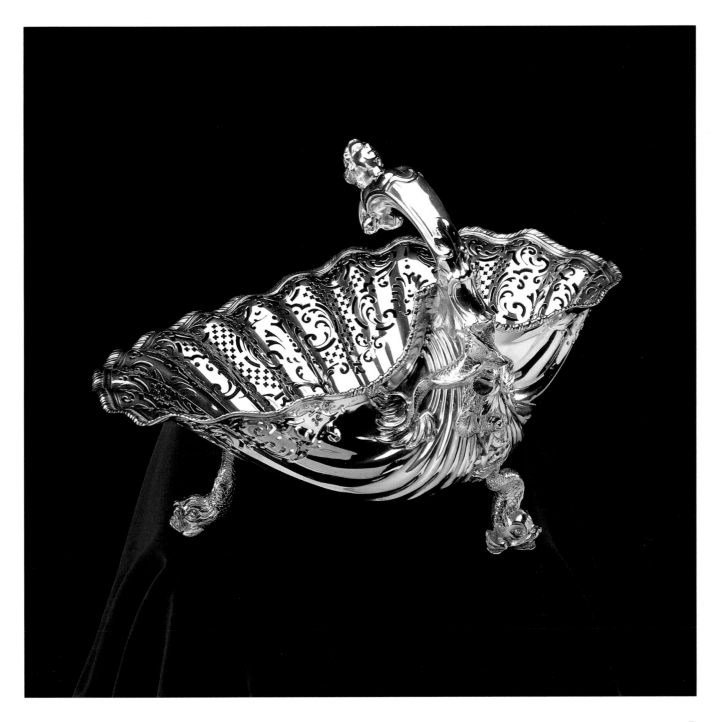

and 1980s adopted a fifty-year rule, so that objects of the 1920s and 1930s could be encompassed. First the artifacts of the late Victorian and Art Nouveau periods became perfectly acceptable, and were then rapidly followed by Art Deco and the products of the immediate prewar period. Now date lines have been virtually abandoned as collectors and dealers focus their attention on newer and newer objects.

Greater flexibility in defining what might be regarded as an antique came not a moment too soon, as the supply of fine-quality pieces produced before 1830 had all but dried up by the 1960s. At the same time, many museums with seemingly unlimited funds were intent on expanding their collections. This meant that the amount of quality antiques available to the market began to dry up, as well as having the unfortunate effect of pushing up the market value of what material was left. Some categories of antiques, such as 16th- and 17th-century silver, early Meissen and Chelsea porcelain, and Ravenscroft glass, soon went beyond the reach of all but the wealthiest collectors. Not only did museums tend to create a shortage of material available to the private collector but, by imaginative and intelligent use of their acquisitions, they heightened the interest of established collectors and laymen alike, thereby increasing the demand for antiques still further.

While this tendency was gathering momentum in the 1960s and 1970s, the growing interest in the private sector was inevitable anyway. A higher level of general prosperity and higher standards of education were only two of the factors which made the public not only more appreciative of all that was best from times past, but also gave them the money to indulge their tastes. Traditionally antique collecting had been the closed preserve of the upper classes, who had the money, the education, and the social background to indulge their tastes. Collecting antiquities developed in Renaissance Italy and spread slowly to more northerly countries. In Britain, for example, the fashion for collecting things of the past only really began to develop in the late 18th century. Emphasis was laid on classical antiquities, fostered by the classical education of the times as well as the acquisitive habits picked up during the obligatory Grand Tour.

From then on, an antiquarian interest in the material objects of the past tended to lag behind by one or two centuries. Thus collectors of the Regency era discovered an interest in Tudor and Jacobean furniture, the Victorians looked to the Restoration and early Georgian period, and the Edwardians had the highest regard for the products of the 18th and early 19th centuries. In general collectors and cognoscente alike disregarded the products of their immediate forebears, which explains why the 1830 rule endured as long as it did.

Interest in collectables has also gone in cycles. There are five- or ten-year highs and lows in different categories, as well as periods of slump due to socio-political and economic factors. Antiques that came on to the market in 1917 or 1942, for example, could be picked up very cheaply. However, people didn't have the money to spend in those years, and there was a general reluctance to invest in material that might be destroyed by enemy action or plundered in the uncertainties of war.

Conversely, the economic upheavals of the late 1960s and early 1970s led to a flight of money out of traditional forms of investment, such as stocks, shares, unit trusts, real estate, and building societies, and into art and antiques. The devaluation of sterling in November 1967 and the subsequent run on the dollar and then the franc created a wave of near hysteria in the antique markets of Europe and America. The leading salerooms reported a 50 percent increase in turnover in the ensuing 12 months alone, right across the board, although in certain categories the turnover was up by as much as 100 percent (for prints and drawings), while silver sales increased by 69 percent.

Coupled with this astonishing increase in sales, it was significant that the leading salerooms on both sides of the Atlantic began diversifying into material of more recent vintage than was generally accepted as antique, and this trend has steadily developed ever since. This even led to the development of separate auction houses, such as Christie's in South Kensington, London, catering specifically to the "newer" antiques, including many articles that would not have been regarded as collectable a few years previously.

The major salerooms, as well as the multitudes of lesser auction houses, were only encouraging a trend that was already there. In the same way, the junk shop of yesteryear has been elevated to the antique shop of today; the weekend junk stall or barrow in a street market has become a booth in a permanent antique market; and the better pieces traded in street markets rapidly move up the scale, with a corresponding mark-up in price at each stage.

As the amount of quality antiques available to the market dwindled, it seemed paradoxical that antique shops were proliferating everywhere at an astonishing rate. The number of good antique shops remained fairly static, nor did they find it any easier to obtain quality material for their stock. The answer to this paradox was, at first, a general lowering of standards; if you clung to increasingly untenable date lines, whether 1830 or 1870, then it was inevitable that you had to settle for second-best or some sacrifice in workmanship, condition, or quality.

The more astute collectors ignored date lines and explored the potential of later material. If the products of the Baroque, Rococo, and Neo-classical periods were no longer available, might not there be much to commend in, say, the products of the Second Empire in France, the Biedermeier era in Germany, or the Victorian era in general?

It was fashionable at one time to write off the entire Victorian period as one of uniformly bad taste. Much of the opprobrium heaped on the bourgeois fashions of the 19th century by subsequent generations was undeserved. It is true that in furniture and art, as in the material comforts of everyday life, the Victorians showed a predilection for the massive, the ornate, and the fussy; but not all was tawdry or tasteless by any means.

That the Victorians were capable of perpetrating, and apparently enjoying, objects of unbelievable hideousness is true, but at the same time there were serious attempts to raise standards. The much-abused Great Exhibition of 1851 did more than is often realized to encourage pride in craftsmanship and demonstrate that a thing could be beautiful as well as functional. Though much that is Victorian was, not so long ago, regarded as hardly worth preserving, there were many other things that possessed enduring qualities, and were recognized as such by discerning collectors, long before such objects had

earned the title or dignity of antique. It has to be added that even the fussy and the florid, the over-ornamented, and the downright ugly from that much-maligned period have acquired a certain period charm.

Conscious efforts to improve public taste and foster pride in workmanship seem like oases in the wilderness of materialism and mass production. In England, the Arts and Crafts Movement inspired by William Morris in the 1880s was an attempt to recapture something of the primeval simplicity in craftsmanship—a reaction against the pomposity and over-ornateness of Victorian taste. It was a precursor of that curious phenomenon at the turn of the century known as Art Nouveau in Britain, as Jugendstil ("youth style") in Germany, or as Liberty style in Italy (from the well-known London department store which was one of its great proponents). The practitioners of the New Art went back to nature for inspiration, and invested their furniture, glass, silver, and ceramics with sinuous lines and an ethereal quality. In turn, this provoked a reaction which resulted in the straight lines of the Bauhaus and the geometric forms associated with Art Deco in the interwar period.

It has to be admitted that these styles and fashions seemed ludicrous to many people at the time, especially in their more exaggerated forms; nevertheless they were the outward expression of a minority in art, in architecture, in furniture, textile, and ceramic design, which strove for improvements (as they saw it) in the production and appearance of objects. These were not only objects intended purely for decorative purposes, but those used in every phase and aspect of life.

The products of the Arts and Crafts Movement, of Art Nouveau, and of Art Deco were despised and neglected in succession, and then, after a decent lapse of time, people began to see them in their proper perspective and appreciate that they had a great deal to offer to the collector.

Nevertheless, it is also fair to comment that the century after 1830 was a barren one as far as the production of fine-quality material was concerned. Thirty years ago collectors made a fine distinction between what was merely old but had no particular merit on grounds of esthetic features or workmanship, and those objects which had some qualities to com-

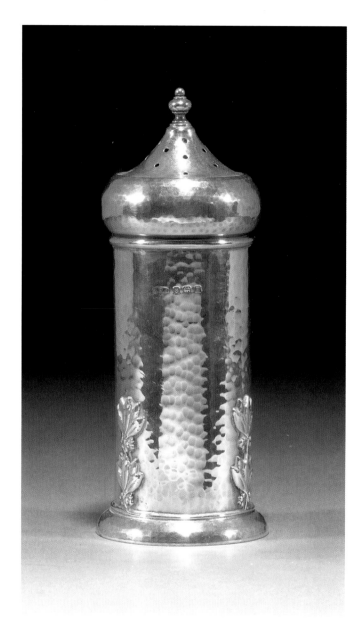

ABOVE: An A.E. Jones silver sugar sifter made in Birmingham in 1929.

mend them. Nowadays, however, as demand continues to outstrip supply, there is a tendency to talk up wares that may be old, but are commonplace and mediocre nonetheless. The insatiable demand especially at the lowest end of the market decrees that this should be so, but it is important for the collector to discriminate and learn to recognize the features and factors that distinguish the worthwhile from the second-rate. Ultimately these are the factors that govern the soundness of any investment in antiques.

In the course of this century there have been startling developments in education, communications, travel, and living standards. Today, people are generally more affluent than were their parents or grandparents. They enjoy shorter working hours and a larger surplus disposable income. Through education and such external stimuli as the cinema and television programs, they have a greater awareness of things of beauty or antiquarian interest. More and more people now have the time and the money to indulge in what was formerly the preserve of a privileged few.

A greater general awareness of what is beautiful and worthwhile inevitably tends to encourage better craftsmanship. Despite the general perception of the period between the two world wars as the nadir in fine design and workmanship there were also many individuals and groups who were active in Europe and America in promoting design consciousness. Today, the products of their studios and workshops, especially in the fields of furniture, ceramics, glass, and metalwork, are deservedly sought after and fetch correspondingly high prices. This trend has continued right down to the present day, with the result that each year the artifacts created by the most imaginative and innovative graduates of the art schools and colleges are eagerly snapped up as the antiques of the future.

Britain, which led the way in the mid 19th century, also pioneered attempts to foster good design in an infinite range of articles, from household appliances to postage stamps, through the medium of the government-sponsored Design Centre and the Council of Industrial Design.

During World War II, when there was a shortage of materials and manpower, these schemes helped to develop the utility concept, which extended over the entire range of manufactured goods. At the time, "utility" was often equated with shoddy and second-rate, but in more recent times collectors have begun to appreciate the simple lines of the applied arts of the so-called austerity period.

There was a time when objects were collected for their own sakes; as examples of exquisite craftsmanship, beauty, or rarity. Perhaps the reason for collecting was nothing more than the charm of owning something of great age. At any rate, intrinsic worth was seldom of primary consideration. Nowadays, however, there is a tendency for the collector to be aware of values and to prize his possessions not only for their esthetic qualities, but also as investments.

Gone are the days of the great gentleman-collectors, such as Sloane, Cotton, Harley, Hunter, Hearst, and Burrell, whose interests covered every collectable medium and whose tastes were equally developed for paintings and incunabula as for coins and illuminated manuscripts. Even the computer billionaires of the present day could scarcely emulate the feat of the late Andrew Mellon, who in the 1920s once purchased 33 paintings from the Hermitage for $19 million. But while there are very few private individuals, who could now afford to buy a Leonardo, a Rembrandt, or even a Van Gogh, there are millions of people throughout the world who have the leisure to specialize in some chosen field, and the surplus cash to acquire the material for their collections. There are countless afficionados who have formed outstanding collections of porcelain, silver, prints, or glass, who have specialized in the products of individual potteries, or Depression glass, or Kilner paperweights or Goss china. At the lower end of the spectrum there are hundreds of different classes of collectable, from the frankly ludicrous, such as bricks, barbed wire, and lavatory chain-pulls, to the fetishistic, including whips and certain articles of ladies' apparel. There are also collectors of commemorative wares and even objects associated with one's profession, such as dental and medical instruments. The collecting virus is now endemic and insatiable. There is any amount of pleasure, and no little profit, to be had from collecting, providing that a sense of proportion is retained and collecting does not become an obsession.

Styles and Periods

For all practical purposes collectable antiques date from the late 15th and 16th centuries. Furniture from this period tends to be massive and made of oak or indigenous timbers such as elm and yew. Chests, stools, small tables, paneled chairs, sideboards, aumbries, wall-cupboards, and refectory tables form the bulk of the furniture. Much of what is described generically as treen comes into this category: wooden trenchers and platters, turned wooden bowls and bread-boards. Cutlery consists largely of bone-handled knives and horn spoons, though horn continued to be used in rural areas well into the 18th century. Pewter dishes, flagons, and tankards are still available, as are broad-bowled pewter spoons. The equivalent in silver, with relatively plain shanks and a flat end, are now elusive and very expensive. Late-medieval glass, mainly imported from Venice, is rare in fine condition. Maiolica pottery, in the form of drug jars, dishes, jugs, and flagons, with polychrome decoration, was produced in Urbino, Faenza, and other Italian towns and exported to northern and western Europe. Here again, good quality maiolica is scarce and worth a king's ransom when it passes through the salesroom. Textile materials include embroidery panels, caps and coifs, gloves, purses, and decorated caskets. Not long ago such material could still be picked up for reasonable sums but, like everything else from this early period, prices are now extremely high.

In the Elizabethan and Jacobean period (approximately 1560–1660) the dominant feature is furniture. Politically and economically, what the Tudors had struggled to accomplish was consolidated in the first half of the 17th century. Although the civil wars and the aftermath of the Commonwealth tend to give the impression of disorder, it was, by and large, a period of rising prosperity and it was the emergence of the wealthy middle classes which precipitated the power struggle with the monarchy.

The styles initiated in furniture during the latter part of the Tudor period were gradually developed during the reigns of the first Stuart kings. It is rather in the expansion of the market that the furniture known as Jacobean stands out from its predecessors. Whereas chairs and tables were hitherto relatively uncommon, a great variety of these objects was developed in the time of James I (1603–25) and Charles I (1625–49). In many respects, Jacobean furniture had the same hallmarks as its Tudor counterparts, but these characteristics were accentuated and carried to their logical conclusion, while the wider variety of objects and the greater quantity manufactured have popularized the label "Jacobean" applied to much of the furniture produced in Britain in the 17th century.

Apart from stools, the Elizabethan household would have boasted few chairs, and many of these would, in effect, have consisted of chests adapted for sitting on. Box seats continued to be fashionable under the Stuarts but were given various refinements such as arms and paneled backs. Gradually the box element was phased out and an open frame adopted, the legs being kept rigid by means of massive stretchers. Joined box-chairs (the Coronation chair in Westminster Abbey is a fine example) had existed since the 14th century, but were confined to the households of the nobility and the wealthiest classes. They only became popular with the poorest classes toward the end of the 16th century and were almost entirely superseded in the Jacobean period by chairs on the open-frame pattern.

Joined furniture developed slowly in the early 1600s. Indigenous timbers, mainly oak, elm, and yew, were used extensively in the production of solid, utilitarian pieces which were evidently built to last. Because of the robust nature of its design a very large proportion of Jacobean furniture has survived to the present day. Curiously enough, a great deal of lighter, upholstered furniture was also manufactured in the same period but this, owing to the perishable nature of the materials involved, has not survived in the same quantity. Chairs and stools of this sort were generally constructed in beech, a type of wood which is particularly prone to attack from furniture beetles and other wood-boring insects. The fabric and stuffing employed did not stand up to hard usage and

it is significant that the few extant examples (mostly existing in museum collections) present a sadly dilapidated appearance.

Furniture produced during the Commonwealth period tended to be more austere and devoid of frivolity. Fine satin fabrics, and even the harder wearing "Turkey" work (so-called because it resembled the Turkish carpets which were beginning to be popular in western Europe at that time) were frowned upon, and the manufacturers substituted leather upholstery secured by large brass-headed nails. After the restoration of 1660 traditional styles continued, but with an increasing amount of decoration. Elaborate punch-work was used on high-paneled backs, often incorporating the date or initials of the owner. Effective use was made of turnery not only in the legs and stretchers but in the smaller supports to the arms of chairs.

In ceramics, Italian maiolica vied with early French faience, but by the end of the 16th century Delft in Holland was an important center for tin-glazed earthenware, mainly blue and white in decoration in imitation of the Oriental porcelains which were now beginning to be imported through the East India Company and its European rivals. In the early 17th century delftware became a generic term for decorative earthenware manufactured at London, Liverpool, Bristol, and Wincanton in England as well as at Dublin, Limerick, and the aptly named Delftfield in Glasgow, each area producing its own distinctive variation. The blue-dash chargers of the late 17th and early 18th centuries are much sought after, not only on esthetic grounds but also for their historic significance, as they are often decorated with portraits of royalty. Mugs, beakers, barbers' basins, bleeding bowls, and apothecaries' jars as well as rack-plates provide ample scope for the collector. Much of this material belongs to a later period, delftware remaining fashionable till the late 18th century.

Soda glass continued to be imported mainly from Venice throughout the Jacobean period and examples in fine condition are now very expensive. The Venetian monopoly was broken by George Ravenscroft who experimented with christalline glass in the Restoration period and by 1675 had evolved an entirely new type of glass containing lead oxide. The lead content was gradually increased and by the beginning of the 18th century had taken on its heavy, dark, brilliant appearance.

In Britain, silver dating before the Restoration is very rare, largely as a result of the civil war period when much of the existing plate was melted down and converted into coin to pay the troops on opposing sides. Small articles, notably spoons, have survived from the Jacobean period but are now very highly priced, especially those decorated with figures of the apostles.

In the Restoration period, which extended to the end of the 17th century and beyond, there was a return to the more florid styles of decoration in furniture, a reaction to the austerely simple lines favored during the Puritan Commonwealth. It should be noted that American colonial furniture of this period tended to retain the simpler lines, influenced by the styles imported by the Pilgrim Fathers in 1620, and this penchant for clean lines and a minimum of decoration continued right through to the Shaker furniture of the 19th century.

Styles in Britain as the 17th century drew to a close were strongly influenced by the Baroque fashions which originated in Italy and spread to Spain, France, and Germany, and which were largely introduced to England by the influx of Huguenot refugees after the revocation of the Edict of Nantes in 1685 increased the persecution of non-Catholics. Baroque (literally the French word for "irregular") was characterised by asymmetrical, curving lines but gradually developed into extravagant and elaborate ornament, festooned with ribbons, scrolls, swags, shells, cornucopias, and cupids. Furniture was not only carved, but often overlaid with gilt gesso work. It was now much lighter in construction, but the craze for curving lines extended to legs and chairbacks. Similar excrescences decorated pottery, glass, and silver.

This period also witnessed the growth of walnut in popularity. Walnut trees had been grown in England since Tudor times but it was not till after the Restoration that it came into fashion as a furniture timber. Even then, the coarse texture of English walnut and its comparative lack of figuring made it less popular than French, Italian, and Spanish walnut, and latterly the black American variety.

The heyday of walnut in English furniture came in the period from 1660–1720, though it remained fairly fashionable as late as the 1760s. The most desirable pieces of walnut furniture now in existence emanate from the later Stuart period during which craftsmen acquired Continental techniques of cabinet-making and produced much elegant furniture with a certain flamboyance characteristic of the Restoration era.

Tremendous impetus to the development of more delicate styles in furniture came in the 1690s; to this period belong the graceful cabinets, chests of drawers, and bookcases which attained their best phase in the reign of Queen Anne (1702–14). When combined with marquetry veneer panels and crossbanding in contrasting timbers such as rosewood, sycamore, and walnut produced highly pleasing decorative effects.

In 1664, the Worshipful Company of Glass-sellers and Looking-glass Manufacturers was incorporated and in the same year George Villiers, second Duke of Buckingham, obtained a patent to make glass. He established a factory at Vauxhall, London, and by the end of the 17th century the production of mirrors had expanded enormously. They continued to be relatively expensive and it was not until about 1740 that they became at all plentiful. Thereafter they became increasingly popular, especially when extravagantly decorated in the Rococo style.

During the same period English pottery began to compete successfully with imported wares although there was nothing to equal the hard-paste porcelain which flooded in from China. The blue and white motifs on Chinese ceramics triggered off a craze for chinoiserie which influenced other forms of the applied arts, from furniture to textiles and metalwork. Certain Oriental decorative arts made a tremendous impact; the fashion for ivory and jade dates from the beginning of the 18th century. Lacquered furniture was introduced to western Europe from the Far East in the latter part of the 16th century, but the wares imported from China and Japan by the Portuguese were relatively minor pieces, mainly chests and small cabinets. Nevertheless the dark glossy appearance of these items was a refreshing change to the dull, massy

ABOVE: An Art Nouveau footed silver rosebowl made in Sheffield in 1910.

furniture which graced the homes of the wealthy classes and it was not long before lacquerware was being imitated in the Low Countries and England.

Oriental lacquer was based on ground varnishes of various colors with lengthy drying periods between many coats which might take up to three years to reach perfection. Western imitators were hampered by lack of the proper materials but by the middle of the 17th century had succeeded in manufacturing a tolerable substitute.

Inevitably japanning, as the European technique was known, failed to achieve the brilliant lustre and durability which characterized Oriental lacquer. The japanning of furniture, however, received great stimulus in 1688 when John Stalker and George Parker published their treatise on japanning and varnishing. In the period from 1690–1730 japanned furniture decorated with chinoiserie was all the rage. Thereafter, it declined in fashion and was virtually eclipsed by 1750 until 1780 when it revived again for a short time and was also briefly in favor in the early 1800s.

Britain emerged as a world power in the early 18th century, after the brilliant successes of its forces in the War of the Spanish Succession. In later conflicts Britain rivaled France for the mastery of the colonial world, in India and the Western Hemisphere and emerged triumphant in 1763. The accession of the Hanoverian kings in 1714 increasingly involved Britain in European politics and artistic influences. Despite the Jacobite rebellions of 1715 and 1745, Britain enjoyed a long period of relative stability and rising prosperity. Greater affluence was reflected in the furniture, silverware, and decorative arts of the period.

The Georgian era is conveniently divided into Early Georgian, covering the reigns of the first two Georges (1714–60), and Late Georgian, corresponding with the long reign of George III (1760–1820). The era as a whole witnessed a tremendous development in architecture which, in turn, influenced styles in the applied and decorative arts. The Early Georgian period coincided with the zenith of the Baroque in Europe, with its emphasis on curves and scrolls in everything from the legs of tables to the handles of coffee pots. Scallops and acanthus leaves decorated the corners and joints of furniture as well as the rims of vessels.

The craze for curved lines culminated in the 1730s with the rise of Rococo, a much lighter, more delicate style than Baroque and clearly a reaction against its tendency to the massive and fussy. The Italianate word was actually derived from two French terms—*rocaille* (rockwork) and *coquille* (shell). It arose out of the vogue for grottoes in landscape gardening and was characterized by floral swags and garlands as well as "C" and "S" curves in great profusion. Britain lagged behind the Continent so it was not until the middle of the century that the Rococo fashion reached its height in England. It lent itself very well to setting off Oriental motifs, later joined by Indian art forms and continued, in a more restrained form, right through to the end of the 18th century. In general Rococo represented a much lighter approach to form and decoration than the baroque. By the end of the century, however, styles were becoming more eclectic, often blending the Rococo with the neo-classical and even the gothic, an artificial revival of certain medieval forms such as pointed arches.

In this period, mahogany and other hardwoods from the Caribbean gradually supplanted walnut as the preferred medium for furniture. Newer shapes and styles included the bombe chest of drawers and the glass-fronted bookcase with broken pediment top. The dominant personality in furniture design in this period was William Kent (1685–1748), the first English architect to include furniture design as an integral part of his interior decoration. On chairs and tables, the technique of "hipping" the legs to the seat or table-top encouraged the ornamentation of the joint. Several motifs were used, among them the cabochon and leaf ornament and the lion, satyr, or human mask being the most popular. The comparative lack of figuring in mahogany was compensated for by the addition of a certain amount of carving, fretting, and piercing, made possible by the greater strength of West Indian hardwoods. This was the great period of the table and the dining table first became widely popular at this time. Smaller, lighter forms, from the folding games table to the sewing table, were also developed in this period and remain immensely popular today.

In glassware this was the period of much lighter forms, encouraged by the Glass Excise Act of 1745 which taxed glass by weight. The massive drinking glasses fashionable in the period from 1685–1720 gave way to the more elegant baluster glasses with knopped stems as the century progressed, and by 1750 became much lighter, the deliberate use of air bubbles (which had originally occurred by accident) leading to air twist stems of amazing intricacy.

Meissen and Sèvres pioneered European porcelain in the first half of the century but it was not until 1750 that the manufacture of similar wares began at Derby, followed by Worcester (from 1751), Chelsea (1745–69), and Bow (1746–76). English bone china rivaled the French and German products in its uniformly high quality in composition, decoration, and potting. There was, of course, a penchant for Chinese and Japanese decoration but European flowers, penciled motifs, armorial features, and transfer-printed ornament were also popular. The shapes favored by the potters were closely modeled on the Rococo styles used by contemporary silversmiths, but there was an enormous demand for figurines, groups, and centerpieces.

The Early Georgian period was the heyday of the great Huguenot silversmith, Paul de Lamerie who embarked on his career in 1712. The early work produced by him is relatively austere in design, the simple forms relieved only by engraving or applied strapwork, fine flat-chasing, and the masks and scrolls so dear to French craftsmen of the late 17th century. As the 18th century progressed, the style of de Lamerie's work was modified considerably and this influenced his contemporaries. During the 1720s, there was a tendency toward greater elaboration, both in shapes and ornament, which found formal expression in the Rococo styles of the following decade. Rococo silver reached its zenith in the decade before de Lamerie's death in 1751 and, as the prime exponent of the style in silver, he was perhaps rather too fond of the massive decoration which characterizes it. Nevertheless his work, with few exceptions, outclassed that of his contemporaries and the discernment of collectors right down to the present ensures that his products fetch very large sums when they turn up in the salesroom.

Devotees of fine English furniture are almost unanimous in the view that the latter half of the 18th century and the opening decades of the 19th marked the zenith of English cabinetmaking. The Late Georgian period witnessed the happy combination of brilliance in design with the perfection in production techniques developed over the centuries, and a wide range of excellent materials never before available in such quantities.

Thomas Chippendale's celebrated *Director*, published in 1754, was only one of the numerous manuals which greatly stimulated good furniture design. Batty and Langley produced their *Treasury of Designs* under the baroque influence of Kent, whereas the *New Book of Ornaments* by Matthias Lock in 1752 favored the Rococo style, and chinoiserie and "gothick" styles found expression in the writings of Matthias Darly and the Halfpennys, William and his son John, in the same period.

The techniques in the manufacture of furniture reached their peak in the same period. Vast improvements in the industry had been made possible by the tremendous growth of the market for good quality pieces which enabled cabinetmakers to expand their businesses and turn over whole sections of their factories to specialisation.

Hitherto, the bulk of the best work was concentrated in the London area, but now the provincial cabinetmakers were emerging as manufacturers of furniture no longer content to ape the fashions of the metropolis (often decades behind) but were producing excellent pieces in the latest fashions and even, as in the case of craftsmen such as Richard Gillow of Lancaster, originating furniture designs for the Londoners to follow. It should not be overlooked either that Thomas Chippendale himself was a Yorkshireman, born at Otley in 1718. After completing his apprenticeship he moved to London and established his workshop there in 1749. Although he dominated English furniture design throughout the second half of the 18th century, other cabinetmakers whose work has been the subject of reappraisal in recent years include his great rivals William Vile and John Cobb, while William Hallett, John Channon, and Pierre Langlois were not far behind. Chippendale and his imitators were at their best when blending the Rococo of Louis Quinze with chinoiserie and the Gothic of Walpole's

RIGHT: A Liberty and Co. silver bowl made in Birmingham in 1937, and a napkin ring.

Strawberry Hill. As well as developing the cabriole leg, they introduced the Chinese claw and ball foot, the straight, angular lines of mid-Georgian, the "Gothick" fretwork leg, and the Chinese lattice back.

In ceramics English craftsmen were also making enormous strides and creating distinctive innovations. This was the era of Josiah Wedgwood, pioneer of Queen's Ware for teasets and other tablewares. Later he turned his attention to various forms of stoneware, first black basaltes and later jasperware in which white cameos and reliefs were set against a ground of pale pastel colors. Both materials were utilised in the production of a huge range of useful and ornamental pottery which laid the foundations of timeless classical lines that remain popular to this day. Many potteries sprang up in this period, competing with each other in the fields of earthenware and soft-paste porcelain. Today, the products of Coalport and Caughley, Lowestoft and Longton Hall, Leeds, New Hall, Rockingham, Spode, Swansea, and Minton have their devotees.

One medium which went through a rather lean time in this period was silver. As a result of its interminable Continental wars, Britain was habitually cut off from the normal sources of supply, and even coinage in this metal was often in short supply. Much of the silver that survives from this period consists of small articles, such as shoe buckles, wine labels, and decorative objects like vinaigrettes and snuff boxes. Wine labels and other small items below 10 dwt in weight were exempt from hallmarking under the Plate Offence Act of 1738 and were therefore marked only on a voluntary and sporadic basis. The Marking Silver Plate Act of 1790, however, stipulated that silver bottle-tickets, whatever their weight, had to be hallmarked.

From then onward silver wine labels present little problem either in dating or in the correct ascription of their manufacturer.

The need for hollowwares that bore a passing resemblance at least to silver induced industrial entrepreneurs like Matthew Boulton of Soho, Birmingham, to apply industrially and on a large scale the techniques of Thomas Bolsover of Sheffield who devised a method of layering copper with a thin sheet of silver. Sheffield plate was widely employed in the manufacture of all manner of objects, from the handles of cutlery and candlesticks to coffee pots, salvers, and tureens. Early Sheffield plate, from 1742 to 1760, was usually tinned on the inner surface, but thereafter silver was applied to both sides. It continued to be fashionable until the 1820s when silver became available in great abundance once more, and it was finally killed off by electroplating which provided a much cheaper and more effective substitute from about 1850 onward.

The Prince of Wales, later King George IV, became Regent in 1811 as a result of the madness of his father who lingered on till 1820. George IV reigned for a decade in his own right and was succeeded by his brother William IV (1830–37). It is convenient, however, to regard this entire period as Regency in terms of style. The Prince Regent's London residence was Carlton House whose interior decoration was entrusted to the architect Henry Holland. Relying largely on French émigré craftsmen, Holland furnished Carlton House in a style which blended classical lines with sumptuous decoration.

To this day "Carlton House" is a generic term to describe all manner of furniture in this neo-classical style. Under the influence of such arbiters of taste as Thomas Hope, furniture gradually became more robust, with greater emphasis on comfort than fragile elegance. In addition to the Oriental and Gothic motifs of an earlier generation such diverse motifs as balloons, classical friezes, and Egyptian elements (inspired by the discovery of the Rosetta Stone and a new-found craze for the archaeology of the Pharaohs) began to make themselves felt. Exotic timbers, especially from the East Indies, became fashionable.

These influences spilled over into ceramics, silver, and glass. Ormolu gilding and Boulle marquetry, pioneered in France, added a touch of the exotic to furniture and all manner of decorative objects. An interesting development in this period was papier mâché, pioneered by Messrs Jennens & Bettridge of Birmingham, to produce small articles ranging from picture and mirror frames to trays and pole-screens. It involved many sheets of paper glued together under great pressure then kiln-dried and lacquered with mother-of-pearl inlay and gilding for decorative effect. At its zenith, around mid century, papier mâché even extended to chests, chairs, and tables.

Regency fashions did not die out abruptly with the accession of William IV in 1830, but already great social and political changes were sweeping over Britain. Although they were not crystallized until the middle of the century, it is customary in the world of fashion to speak of the Victorian era as if it had commenced seven years before the young queen ascended the throne in 1837. While fashion in ceramics, glass, and silver did not change much before the Great Exhibition of 1851, the styles, techniques, and even the materials of furniture had been undergoing radical alteration in previous decades. The rapid growth of economic prosperity, which came in the 1830s, stimulated a tremendous demand for furniture.

Overnight the traditional craft of furniture making was transformed into a major industry. Mechanical devices and the labor saving techniques of mass production were introduced to accelerate output. Unfortunately furniture in that period did not lend itself well to mass production and inevitably the standards of craftsmanship, and the enduring qualities which one looks for in good cabinetmaking, were sacrificed in the process.

Because the traditional timbers, oak, beech, elm, yew, walnut, and imported hardwoods such as mahogany and rosewood, were not really suitable for mechanized furniture making, pine and other softwoods were used increasingly, especially for cheap, painted furniture. This was also the era in which the retail furniture supplier emerged, who bought vast quantities of chairs, tables, beds, and wardrobes from the wholesalers who, in turn, got them from the factory. The direct contact between the furniture maker and the consumer was almost totally eliminated. This pattern of furniture production and distribution has continued down to the present day and was economically inevitable.

The old method of direct contact between manufacturer and consumer was not entirely extinguished. Where it survived, the best traditions of custom-built pieces were maintained, and examples of furniture made to a specific order after 1830 may be as interesting and desirable to the connoisseur as anything produced before that date. It is interesting to note that American furniture, which in colonial times and for half a century thereafter had slavishly followed the styles of the erstwhile mother country, and relied heavily on English imports, now began to develop along distinctive lines, and before the century was out would be exerting its own influence on style. The Shaker furniture of the 19th century, in fact, would have a seminal effect on the developments of the 20th century in which form and functionalism took priority over ornament.

Victorian silver, characterized as so much else from that ebullient era by its extravagant and ostentatious use of decoration, was arguably the most derided and despised aspect of the 19th century applied arts. Silver was the most important status symbol of the Victorian period and, for those who could afford it, it was impossible to have too much of a good thing. As a result of the discovery of vast silver deposits in America and Australia the output of the raw material increased enormously to meet the demand created by rising prosperity in the United States, Britain, and western Europe. The period from 1830–1900 was a boom time for the silver industry. The restrained classicism of the silver produced in the Regency period, exemplified by the earlier works of Paul Storr and the other great artist-craftsmen of the time, gave way in the 1830s to the Rococo revival. In place of simple gadrooning and Egyptian ornament, came the asymmetrical lines and scrollwork of the Rococo style but, as so often the case in revivals, the craze for rocaille was taken to extremes.

The straightforward acanthus leaf motif of Regency silver gave way to trailing vines and a veritable tangle of scrollwork. Bases became massive and rock-like and the emphasis was laid on the weight or massy appearance of the object. Here and there, however, were examples of simple yet elegant pieces, mainly table wares, and these have generally held their value better than the fussy centerpieces and presentation pieces.

Although Victorian is used as a generic term for the applied and decorative arts of the 19th century it had its European counterparts. The Biedermeier furniture and decor of mid-19th century Germany was long derided—indeed, the term was derived from a fictional character, Gottlieb Biedermeier, a rather simple-minded, essentially philistine petit-bourgeois—as conventional and unimaginative, but today its very solidity is now regarded as highly commendable, while there is much to delight the eye in many of the lesser pieces, especially the ceramics, glass, and silver. The French equivalent was Second Empire, roughly contemporary with the reign of Napoleon III (1852–71), and likewise unfairly dismissed by the generations that followed immediately.

As the 19th century drew to a close, influences and developments in the applied and decorative arts became much more cosmopolitan. The French expression *fin de siecle* has come to be synonymous with decadence. The estheticism expressed by Oscar Wilde, J.K. Huysmans, and Robert de Montesquieu had its parallels all over Europe and even extended to America. The strange, exotic, luxuriant, and faintly decadent spirit of the times had its flowering in the sinuous lines of Art Nouveau. It was a period of eclecticism, when artists and designers drew freely on all the artistic styles and movements of previous generations from every part of the world, and often jumbled them together in a riotous compote. The craze for Japanese art and artifacts was predominant, but inspiration was also derived from the ancient civilizations of Greece and Rome, Persia, India, Peru, Mexico, Benin, and China. Nevertheless, it is significant that the German term for the turn of the century developments in the arts was Jugendstil or "youth style," implying vigor, freshness, originality, and modernity. The followers of the Arts and Crafts Movement, on the one hand, rejected modern mass production techniques and sought to return to first principles, to handicrafts and inspiration from nature; the disciples of Jugendstil, on the other hand, did not spurn the machine if it could be used to their advantage, and they looked forward, in an age of speed

LEFT: An English silver lidded flagon of 1675 with a short molded lip added about 1725. Its interest is considerably increased by the lengthy presentation inscription to Sir Edmund Berry Godfrey engraved on its side.

and light, to producing works which would express the qualities of the age.

The major countries of Western Europe and the United States each had an important part to play in the development of the applied and decorative arts. In Britain, the desire for improvement in industrial design can be traced back to the Great Exhibition of 1851 and, even earlier, to the Royal Commission on the Fine Arts in 1835. The Gothic Revival of the mid 19th century stimulated interest in medievalism, reflected in the religious overtones of the early work of William Morris, Philip Webb, and Edward Burne-Jones. It would be difficult to overestimate the importance of Morris to the artistic development of Britain in the late 19th century. Two important movements stemmed directly or indirectly from his teachings, the Arts and Crafts Movement of the 1880s which aimed at bringing artists and craftsmen closer together, to raise standards of workmanship and to put artistic pride into even the most mundane articles, and the Aesthetic Movement, founded on an elitist principle which genuinely strove to raise standards of design and taste. On the continent of Europe, the styles which culminated in Art Nouveau had their origins in France where two major artistic movements flourished in the last third of the century, Naturalism and Symbolism. There were parallel developments in Belgium, Italy, and Spain which fused in the 1890s, were enthusiastically adopted in England and given a distinctly British flavor before finding their way back across the Channel in the guise of *le style anglais*.

The Civil War of 1861–65 was no less traumatic for the United States than the German occupation and the Commune of 1870–71 were for France. The rapid expansion of industry, coupled with widespread immigration from Europe, changed the character of the country in the last three decades of the century. America ceased to be a pioneer land and in the aftermath of the Spanish-American War of 1898 assumed an imperial role. In the arts, as in politics, America now reached out to every part of the globe. Interest in the arts of China and Japan, of Latin America and Africa, were combined with the traditional styles which were themselves derived from the British, Dutch, and German of the colonial era or imported with the waves of European migration from the 1860s onward. This blend of Oriental or pre-Columbian influences with the styles and techniques of Europe could be seen in the furniture, glassware, and ceramics of America at the turn of the century. These, especially art glass and studio pottery, found their way to Europe where they exerted a considerable influence on the applied arts of the present century.

The young architects and designers of the Chicago School revolutionized the design of buildings and furniture from the 1890s onward. In Europe, the break with the old ideas was often more dramatic as, for example, in the Sezession movement in Austria and Germany. The world of arts and crafts was thrown into turmoil. Many new ideas and styles appeared; some were short-lived and have now become crystallized in the history of the period, but others contained the seeds that germinated in the 1920s and came to full maturity nearer the present day, notably the Bauhaus movement in Germany which influenced the development of Art Deco in the 1920s, with its rejection of the curvilinear extravagance of Art Nouveau. Geometric forms and bright primary colors were in tune with the Jazz Age. Many new forms emerged in the interwar period; the cigarette lighter and the powder compact replaced the snuff-box and vinaigrette of earlier generations as ornamental objects which have since become eminently collectable.

While the main collectable categories through the different styles and periods have concentrated on furniture, ceramics, silver, and glass, it should be noted that many other, minor categories emerged mainly in the 19th and 20th centuries and now merit the serious attention of collectors. Although medieval textiles, mainly in the form of needlework, occasionally turn up, the great bulk of material in this category consists of costume from the 18th century onward, with the emphasis on items of apparel from the late 19th and 20th centuries. While clocks and barometers, for practical collecting purposes, exist from the early 18th century onward, relatively few scientific instruments available to the collector predate 1800. Watches, cameras, and optical instruments are even later in origin. Glass paperweights, often produced with the odds and ends left over at the end of the day, have only been around for about a century and half. Few children's playthings date before 1800; the majority of dolls and mechanical toys that now pass through the salesrooms date from 1850 while teddy bears go back no further than the early 1900s. In recent years new categories have attracted a wide following and range from car mascots and aviation memorabilia to golfing, angling, and other sporting collectables.

Pitfalls and Plus Factors

Collectors, and not always beginners by any means, are often puzzled by the vast price differential between two objects which are superficially similar. In some cases there may be as many as a dozen criteria governing the value of an object: age, materials, type of construction, quality of craftsmanship, artistic or esthetic considerations, unusual technical or decorative features, the provenance of personal association, the presence or absence of makers' marks, full hallmarks, dates, and inscriptions. These and other criteria vary in importance from one object to another, and may even vary within the range of a single category, at different periods or in certain circumstances. Visiting museums and stately homes or handling actual objects at sale previews, as well as studying all the available specialist literature on any given subject, will help the aspiring collector to get a feel for the subject, but there is no short cut to gaining expertise.

Above all, condition is the most problematic factor in assessing the worth of an object. Reasonable condition, of course, depends on the object and the degree to which damage and repairs are accepted by specialist collectors and dealers. A very fine early paneled chair might well have a replacement to the last two inches of a back leg and, if well done, this would have practically no effect on the price. On the other hand, a run-of-the-mill lacquer object, scratched and crudely repainted, would be almost valueless. The general rule is that where a piece is interesting and few collectors have one in their collection, a much damaged example will fetch a surprisingly good price.

This often happens with early examples of ceramics from important factories, whereas a common jug, missing a handle,

will be virtually worthless. The failure to appreciate the effects on value of poor condition, which of course includes lack of patination, loss of original surface, fading, fraying, or rubbing, is one of the most common causes of the misunderstanding that arise between collectors and dealers.

The market value will also take into account the imponderables of where, when, and how an article came on to the market. There is often a wide disparity in the sum which identical objects may fetch in a London salesroom, in a provincial auction, or a country house sale. The individual vagaries of obsessiveness of two or more wealthy private collectors may grossly affect the auction prices of certain objects on a particular occasion, while absolutely identical objects can (and sometimes do) fetch half these sums at other times in other places. Moreover, there is both a greater disparity between prevailing auction realizations and dealers' retail prices in general, and between the prices of one dealer and another—not always miles apart! Unfortunately, the collector cannot shop around before making a purchase. There are still bargains to be picked up; but all too often one finds that objects are outrageously overpriced in general antique or junk shops. Contrary to popular belief, some of the keenest bargains are still to be found in metropolitan antique shops and markets, where competition comes into play; conversely some of the most atrocious overpricing has been observed in provincial towns or the antique boutiques in tourist areas. There is no clearly definable regional pattern of pricing in the United Kingdom or the United States or anywhere else for that matter; this is something which collectors have to explore themselves.

While a certain amount of judicious repair and restoration is permissible, fakery is reprehensible and usually detracts from whatever value the genuine part of the object may have had before it was tampered with. Unfortunately the dividing line between legitimate repair and outright faking is often a rather tenuous one, but the general principle is that any deliberate altering of an object to create something of greater value is a form of fraud. It occurs most often in furniture where large but unfashionable and unsaleable pieces are dismembered and their timbers used to recreate small pieces which, with a bit of luck, can be passed off as genuine articles. The other problem which besets the unsuspecting collector is reproduction. During the Gothic Revival of the early 19th century some cabinetmakers produced passable reproductions of Jacobean oak and these sometimes present a problem. As a rule, however, the tools used in planing or cutting the timber, or the methods of joining, even where some attempt is made to copy the original, are the factors which reveal the truth. In any case, early Victorian reproductions of earlier styles are now regarded as antiques in their own right, although there will obviously be quite a wide difference in the antiquarian value. So too with early 20th century reproductions of Louis Quinze.

In porcelain it is often a greater problem especially where such factories as Meissen, Derby, or Worcester revive old patterns. Generally speaking, however, variations in marking help to distinguish between the originals and the revivals. In all such cases of doubt, it is recommended that the would-be purchaser get the advice of a reputable dealer or auctioneer. Legislation in many countries in recent years, such as the Trades' Descriptions Act in Britain, place a grave responsibility on the vendors and their agents to ensure that articles are properly described.

At the end of the day, the age-old maxim *caveat emptor* is as important as ever, but do not let this deter you from enjoying the quest for your chosen subject. All collectors make mistakes along the way but so long as they learn from the experience no great harm is done.

The History of Silver

Flatware

This is the generic term for sets of forks and spoons, from the fact that they were produced from flat strips of metal. Spoons existed as separate items long before the introduction of forks in the 17th century, but this led to the production of sets of forks and spoons, with handles of uniform design. Sets of flatware began to appear about 1660 and thenceforward can be dated by their shape, design, and technical features. Flatware was produced in silver, less commonly in pewter, and in Sheffield plate from about 1770, and electroplate from 1840 onward.

The earliest style for individual pieces is the trefid pattern, where forks have two or three prongs and knives a cannon handle. The dog-nose, wavy end, and shield end patterns were fashionable in the early 18th century, and forks were still three-pronged. The Hanoverian pattern, popular from 1710 onward, at first had a rat-tail on the back of spoon bowls but this feature was replaced in about 1730 by a single or double drop at the junction of bowl and handle. The Old English pattern (1760–1800) was noted for long, slim, tapering stems and four-pronged forks. This was the first pattern for which complete services (all pieces by the same maker in the same year) became available, although full services are rare. Other patterns in this period were the Onslow (1760–80) with a distinctive scroll end cast separately and soldered on with a sleeved joint, and the feather-edged pattern (1770–80), distinguished by a narrow border of diagonal cuts. A beaded edge, followed by a reeded edge, was popular from 1790 to 1810.

The fiddle pattern dominated the first half of the 19th century, stems and handles being shaped like a fiddle. Variations included the fiddle, thread, and shell pattern with a shell motif on the ends of handles. Hour-glass or king's pattern was similar but with a more pronounced waist. Queen's pattern (1840-70) was heavier and had convex fluting on the shell motif. Later flatware tended to repeat or modify existing patterns, and decorative features were a plus factor.

Collectors distinguish flatware in early and later Sheffield plate. The former (1760–1800) has bowls struck from sheet metal, the backs and fronts of forks being stamped separately. The latter (1800–40) has bowls struck from dies soldered, to stems die-struck from thick plated metal sheet and edges hammered to a fine bevel to conceal the exposed copper.

Decorative features such as scrollwork and lacy pattern on early types of flatware are rare and worth a good premium. Full hallmarking on flatware up to 1790 is very desirable, though this feature is rare on early knife handles. Provincial variations exist and are worth seeking out. Distinctive modifications of standard patterns were produced in Scotland and Ireland and are only now beginning to be really appreciated.

Hollowwares

This is the generic term for silver vessels (cups, tankards, bowls, teapots, and so on) which were beaten up from sheets of metal into a hollow form, though latterly most pots and tankards were cut from sheet metal soldered at the edges and bases. Relatively little silver predating 1660 has survived, as the majority of pieces would have been melted down for coinage during the Thirty Years War (1618–48) or the English Civil Wars (1642–48) and similar upheavals of the 17th century. Tudor and Jacobean silver, and its Continental counterparts, was relatively simple in form, with little or no ornament. By the late 17th century, however, decoration was coming into fashion, in the form of embossing and repousse work on sheet silver or chasing and chiselling on silver cast for bases, handles, and rims. Die-stamping, whereby complete articles could be formed by drop-forging under high pressure, was developed in the 18th century and widely used for all manner of silver pots, bowls, and baskets as well as dishes. Engraving was applied to flat surfaces, especially trays and salvers, but was increasingly employed on pots, caddies, and tankards and reached its zenith in the late 18th century, allied to such techniques as bright-cutting, faceting, piercing, and fretting. In the same period, other ornamental effects were achieved by cut-card work, in which floral patterns were cut from thin sheets of silver and soldered to the surface of vessels, often in combination with cast beading. Guilloche or engine-turning was a technique developed in the early 19th century to create spiral and criss-cross patterns of engraving on surfaces.

Those who could not afford solid gold articles made do with silver-gilt, a technique which was also applied to vessels holding fruit whose acidity would otherwise have corroded the metal. Sometimes pieces were partially gilded (parcel-gilt) to produce an effective contrast between decorative relief and the background. As well as useful wares for the table, such as dishes, plates, bowls, tureens, teapots, coffee pots, sugar bowls, tankards, flagons, serving dishes, casters, and condiment sets, there are numerous decorative articles such as candlesticks and candelabra, epergnes, and centerpieces.

A strict control over the use and manufacture of silver in England since medieval times evolved into a system of hallmarks, symbols which give the date and place of assay as well as identifying the maker. Though generally reliable, it should be noted that marks have been forged, while fakes have been created by grafting a piece with genuine hallmarks on to a vessel, perhaps of a much later period. Sometimes, however, this trick was practiced by silversmiths to evade the tax payable at the time of hallmarking. For these reasons it is always advisable to buy silver from a reliable dealer or salesroom. European and American silver was not always marked, although any imported into Britain required to be assayed and taxed accordingly.

Candlesticks

Although made in many parts of central and western Europe from the Middle Ages onward, candlesticks for the collector practically date from the mid 17th century. The pricket candlestick, characterized by its conical spike on which the candle was impaled, gave way to the socket candlestick during the 17th century, but examples are of the greatest rarity. Socket candlesticks, though in existence from about 1500, did not become fashionable until 1650. Thereafter candlesticks became increasingly popular and a wide variety of types were produced in the 18th and 19th centuries.

From about 1840 onward, however, styles became mixed and eclectic, and there is a considerable vogue at the present day for period reproductions. Candlesticks today have taken on ornamental, as opposed to actual, functions and the situation is further confused by the unfortunate practice of converting genuine candlesticks to take electric light, and by the cannibalisation of pieces from different candlesticks, which are sometimes of widely varying periods.

The earliest collectable types have a wide grease-pan halfway up the stick and a flat, spool- or trumpet-shaped base. A very short, squat type was popular in the late 18th century and had the grease-pan mounted on a tall circular base. A characteristic feature of this type was the rectangular slot in the side of the socket so that candle-stubs could be ejected. The earliest sticks had solid stems but Huguenot craftsmen about 1690 introduced stems hollow-cast in two halves and joined by brazing. Relatively plain octagonal bases were fashionable in the early 1700s but by 1720 faceting had become popular. Hexagonal and later square bases were in vogue. The grease-pan disappeared by 1690 and was replaced by an enlarged socket rim. From this evolved the sconce, a detachable rim for catching wax drips, which came into use in the 1720s.

Silver candlesticks can be precisely dated by their hallmarks, but examples in brass, pewter, or bronze can be dated by the shape of their stems and bases which became more elaborate as the 18th century progressed. Square bases with chamfered corners (1725–35) were followed by scalloped or petalled bases (1735–50) which are more or less circular in form. In the same period baluster stems became more elaborate and the number of knops (rings) increased. About 1770 sticks became taller and more elegant. The neo-classical sticks of 1790–1830 may be recognized by their square or octagonal bases, relatively high, with tall, slender, slightly tapered stems characterized by fluting and gadrooning. Late 19th century sticks imitated earlier styles, though the Aesthetic candlestick, designed by Philip Webb for Liberty with a consciously medieval aspect, was highly distinctive and now very desirable.

Small silver

There is an enormous range of small silver articles which appeal to collectors on account of their relative size and inexpensiveness. A major problem with the earlier pieces is that many British pieces bear no hallmarks since items weighing less than 10 dwt were exempt from assay until 1790. In this category come shoe and belt buckles, buttons, thimbles, and wine labels, although most of them have makers' marks or initials which are a help in establishing date and attribution. Larger items should be fully hallmarked and boxes should have marks on both the main box and the lid.

Silver snuff boxes were fashionable throughout the 18th and 19th centuries, and the earliest types (1720–60) had a close-fitting lid which fits all round and lifts off in use. Oval boxes are worth more than those of a rectangular shape with a scalloped edge. Later boxes have hinges with three to five knuckles and lugs, the more the better. Their value depends on size, decoration, maker, condition, and the presence of presentation inscriptions. Novelty boxes in the form of ladies' shoes or a fox's mask, command a good premium.

Vinaigrettes were small silver boxes designed to hold pieces of sponge soaked in acetic acid and aromatic spices as an antidote to contagious diseases. In practice the strongly smelling mixture would have counteracted the foetid stench in an age when personal hygiene was virtually non-existent. These little boxes became popular in the 1780s but were superseded in the 1860s by the double-ended scent bottle. These boxes are easily identified by their heavily gilded interiors and the presence of a perforated inner lid to hold the sponge in place. There are many floral patterns and novelty shapes but the most desirable are the pictorial and commemorative types.

Silver thimbles were produced mainly in the 18th and 19th centuries; those with scenery and landmarks or commemorative motifs are the most desirable, while examples inlaid with gold are rare. Wine labels date from about 1740 and went through various forms—shield, broad rectangular, crescent, eye, and oval and latterly (1820–60) fancy shapes with animal forms and vine-leaves as prime favorites. Labels with the names of unusual or long-obsolete wines rate a high premium.

Silver stamp boxes evolved in the 1840s when postage stamps were imperforate and had to be cut up ready for use, but they survived well into the 20th century. The smallest variety were shaped like envelopes and often mounted with a ring for attachment to a watch-chain or chatelaine, but there were many different desk types in the form of small boxes with one or more glazed lids into which stamps of different denominations could be inserted. Patent dispensers and stamp moisteners were also produced in silver and have a strong philatelic following.

Charles II Trefid Spoon
c.1674

At a Glance

Date: c.1674
Origin: England
Brief description: A Charles II trefid spoon with the initials "C.I.A." engraved on the back, by Lawrence Coles.

Before the middle of the 17th century knives and spoons were made individually, and forks were a relatively new-fangled introduction from Italy. Cutlery was not produced in matched sets before about 1660 when the technique of stamping out knives, forks, and spoons from sheets of metal was adopted.

The first distinctive pattern, which continued until the end of the 17th century, was the trefid pattern, so-called on account of the three lobes at the end of the handle. This spoon dating from about 1674 bears the maker's mark of Lawrence Coles who flourished in London in the decades following the Restoration of 1660. The spoon bears the scratched initials "C.L.A." which would probably have identified the original owner, and alludes to the fact that, at that period, people tended to keep their own separate set of cutlery.

Slip-top Spoons
1630–52

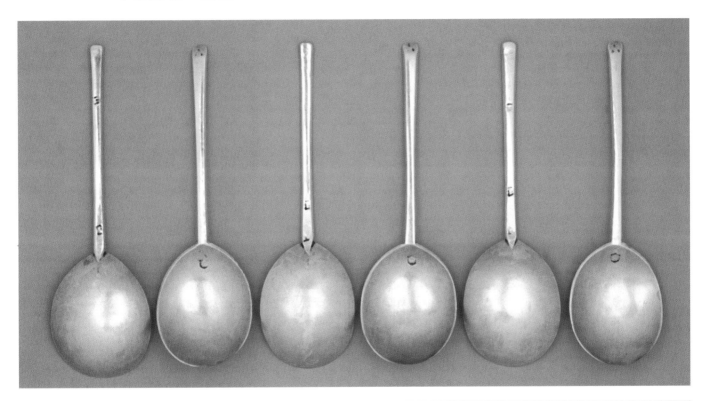

Early silver spoons were confined to the upper classes but tended to be personal items carefully treasured and for that reason they have survived. The earliest spoons had fig-shaped bowls and long narrow stems terminating in a tiny knop or a diamond point, but by the 14th century they had acquired a slip top and this style remained fashionable until the mid 17th century. Some research into the identities of GSS and TW—the initials engraved on the spoons—would enhance the value.

At a Glance

Date: 1630–52

Origin: England

Brief description: Six slip-top spoons with deep-shaped bowls whose reverse has been pricked with a stylized cypher, possibly TW. The tops are engraved with the initials GSS. One bears the assay mark for 1630 but the maker's mark is indistinct, while the other five are by Jeremy Johnson, 1652.

Jacobean and Early Georgian Cutlery
1673–1714

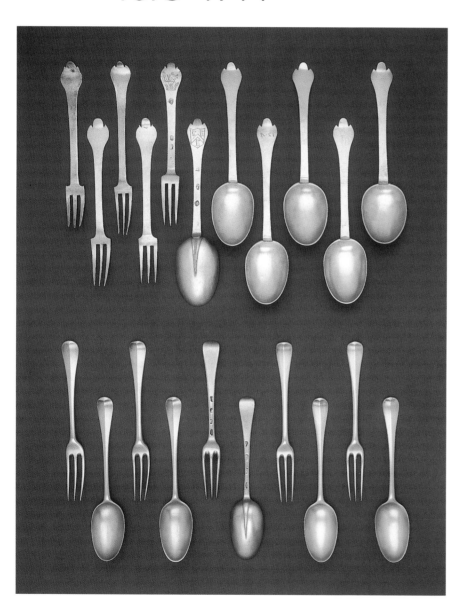

At a Glance

Date: 1673–1714
Origin: England
Brief description: A set of six James II silver trefid-end spoons, a selection of Charles II silver treffid-end forks, and a rare set of 18 George I silver-gilt dessert spoons and matching dessert forks by Philip Robinson, 1714.

Spoons existed as separate items until the early 17th century when forks were introduced to England from Italy. Thereafter they were often produced in matching pairs or sets with handles of a uniform design. Sets of flatware began to appear about 1660 following the Restoration and later on they can be dated by their shape, design, and technical features. The earliest form had a trefid (three-lobed) end to the handles, typified in this set of six James II trefid-end spoons, 1686; a pair of Charles II trefid-end forks, 1673 and three trefid-end forks of 1675, 1680, and 1681. The picture also includes (below) a rare set of 18 George I silver-gilt dessert spoons and matching dessert forks by Philip Robinson, 1714.

Georgian Cutlery
1740–1816

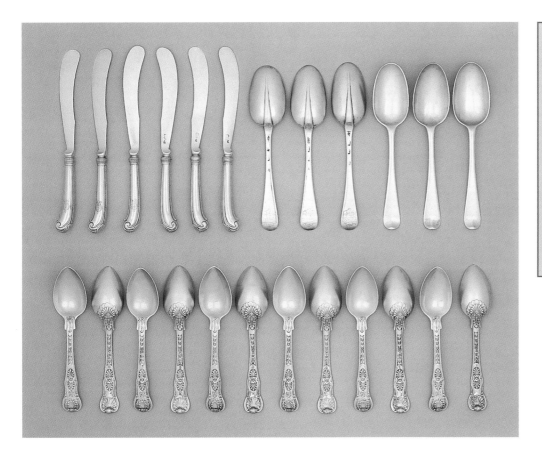

At a Glance

Date: 1740–1816
Origin: England
Brief description:
A set of six George II silver-gilt dessert knives (top left); a set of six George I silver-gilt Hanoverian pattern spoons (top right); and a set of 12 George III silver-gilt dessert spoons (below).

The most celebrated English silversmith of the early 18th century was Paul de Lamerie, son of a Huguenot refugee. His early work was relatively austere but by the 1720s it was becoming increasingly elaborate. The florid Rococo ewers and salvers of his later period are now beyond the reach of most collectors, but his pistol-handled knives and other flatware are still relatively reasonable. The other great Paul of English silver is Paul Storr (1771–1844) who also worked in the Rococo style and dominated the Regency period. The set of six George II silver-gilt dessert knives with plain scimitar blades and reeded pistol grips are by Paul de Lamerie, 1740; the set of six George I silver-gilt Hanoverian pattern table spoons are by de Lamerie, 1719; and the set of 12 George III silver-gilt double shell and laurel pattern dessert spoons are by Paul Storr, 1813–16.

Hour-glass Pattern Dessert Service
1804–80

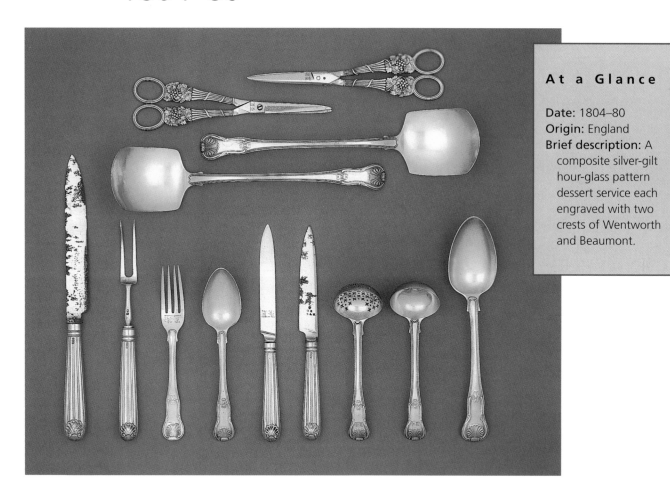

At a Glance

Date: 1804–80
Origin: England
Brief description: A composite silver-gilt hour-glass pattern dessert service each engraved with two crests of Wentworth and Beaumont.

The entire dessert service comprises some 152 pieces of different periods and patterns, whose only unifying factor is the fact that they once belonged to the same family and were at various times engraved with the crests of Wentworth and Beaumont. As well as various sizes of spoons, fruit knives, and forks, the service includes grape scissors, ice spades, a sifting spoon, and ladle, all in a fitted brass-bound case. The pieces are by various makers, from Eley & Fearn (1804) to Francis Higgins (1880).

Bateman and Traies Table Services
1816–83

At a Glance

Date: 1816–83
Origin: England
Brief description:
Two table services:
a King's pattern
table service, mostly
William Bateman
1816; and a William
IV fiddle and
shell pattern
table service, mostly
William Traies.

The somewhat eclectic nature of the flatware used in most upper-class households is typified by these two table services. The king's pattern table service is mostly by William Bateman (1816), but includes pieces by Eley & Fearn, William Chawner, and Moses Brent. The William IV fiddle and shell pattern table service by William Traies, 1831, has 20 teaspoons by Higgins, 1883. The Bateman family of London silversmiths were prominent throughout the 18th and early 19th centuries. Best-known was the redoubtable Hester Bateman (1708–94) who trained under her husband John but after his death she carried on the business and raised it to new heights, ably assisted by her sons Peter and Jonathan, her daughter-in-law Ann, and especially her grandson William who took the family's tradition for superlative craftsmanship through to the Victorian era.

Francis Higgins Table Service
1860

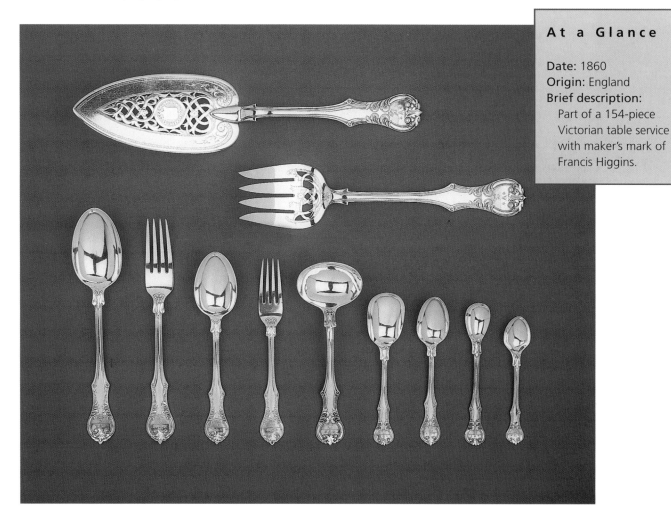

At a Glance

Date: 1860
Origin: England
Brief description:
   Part of a 154-piece
   Victorian table service
   with maker's mark of
   Francis Higgins.

This table service is arguably a fine example of Victorian vanity and was probably commissioned to celebrate the elevation of its proud possessor to the ranks of the gentry. It was manufactured by Francis Higgins, 1860, and includes fish slice and fork, soup ladle, basting spoons, salt and mustard spoons as well as a full range of knives, forks, and spoons, all engraved with the arms granted to Joseph Pearse in March 1860.

Adams Fish Serving Cutlery
1872

At a Glance

Date: 1872
Origin: England
Brief description: A cased Victorian fish serving fork and knife with the mark of George Adams.

Special implements for serving fish are thought to have originated in Germany or Scandinavia by the 1720s, although they did not begin to appear in the British Isles until around the middle of the 18th century. The Earl of Kildare in 1745 is believed to have been the first person to commission a special "trowel" for this purpose, but certainly by 1751 special trowels for serving puddings and fish were being listed by the Goldsmiths' Company and they rapidly became fashionable from then onward. Although they often formed part of a large dinner service, they were often produced as a pair comprising a fish slice and fork as a cased set. This pair, by George Adams (1872) has handles of naturalistic form with fish and seaweed on a granulated ground and a shell terminal.

Ashbee Butter Knife

1901

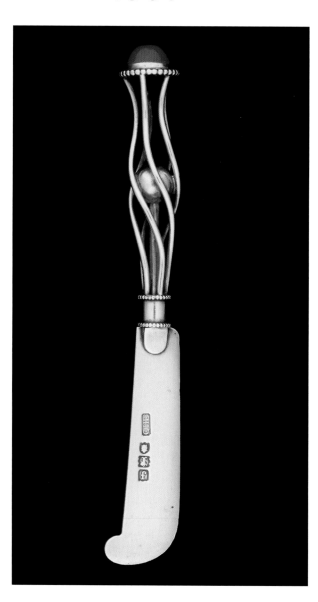

At a Glance

Date: 1901
Origin: England
Brief description:
A silver and chrysoprase
butter knife designed by C.R.
Ashbee and made by the
Guild of Handicraft.

This butter knife with its distinctive twisted openwork handle
and cabochon chrysoprase finial, was designed by Charles
Robert Ashbee (1863–1942), an architect and interior designer
who made a tremendous impact on the Arts and Crafts
Movement, although later he realized that machinery and
mechanical processes were inevitable. He was the founder of
the Guild of Handicraft in London, later relocated to the
Cotswolds, and it was in its workshops that this knife was
produced in 1901.

Mappin and Webb Table Service
1911

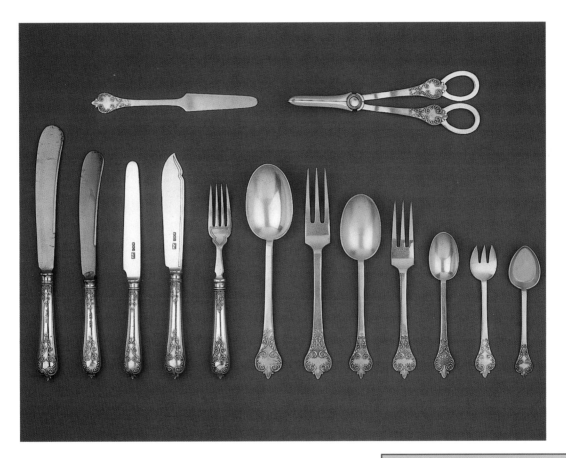

The handles are stamped with foliage, the spoons have lace-back bowls and the forks three prongs, by Mappin and Webb, 1911. The service includes pickle forks, oyster forks, sauce ladles, grape scissors, and gilt-bowl ice spoons. This is a good example of the astonishing endurance of the traditional trefid-end pattern, which remains popular to this day. The hallmarks, of course, are the true test of the actual date of manufacture.

At a Glance

Date: 1911
Origin: England
Brief description: Part of a 500-piece trefid-end pattern table service by Mappin and Webb.

Charles Rennie Mackintosh Cutlery Set
1902

This cutlery was one of 12 sets designed by Mackintosh for Francis Newbury, principal of the Glasgow School of Art, and later divided among his descendants. Charles Rennie Mackintosh (1869–1928) is regarded today as one of the leading figures in the Art Nouveau movement at the turn of the 19th century. He trained as an architect and designed the Glasgow School of Art, as well as a number of churches, schools, private houses, and the famous tearooms operated by Miss Cranston. He designed fixtures and fittings, furniture, and all aspects of the applied arts, including cutlery.

At a Glance

Date: 1902
Origin: Scotland
Brief description: A set of four spoons and forks with pointed oval finials designed by Charles Rennie Mackintosh and made by A.D.W. Hislop of Glasgow.

Caddy Spoons
19th–20th centuries

At a Glance

Date: 19th–20th centuries
Origin: Great Britain
Brief description: A selection of early
silver caddy spoons.

*Small spoons for ladling tea out of the
caddy are characterized by a
comparatively large and shallow bowl
and a very short handle. There is a
considerable variety in the shape of
the bowls, from the scalloped shell to
leaf, scoop, shovel, or pear-shaped,
fluted, or circular types. Handles range
from the slim and elegant to the short
and stubby and many of them were
cast in fancy animal or floral shapes.*

Blacet Dessert Service
1809–19

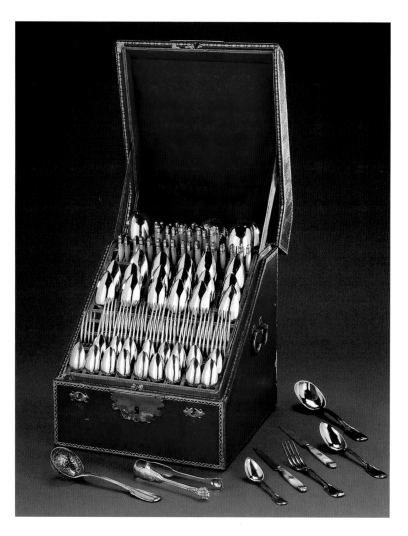

At a Glance

Date: 1809–19
Origin: France
Brief description: A silver-gilt dessert service, the majority with the mark of Louis François Blacet, in a fitted case.

The majority of the pieces in this case bear the mark of Louis François Blacet, a Parisian silversmith. The handles are of the fiddle and thread pattern, each engraved with the initials "E.C." within a shield and foliage sprays. The service comprises dessert spoons, forks and knives, serving spoons, two sifting spoons, sugar-tongs, and an assortment of teaspoons. The fruit knives have silver-gilt blades while the knives have silver-gilt mounted mother-of-pearl handles.

Keller Table Service
c.1900

The complete service consists of tablespoons, table forks, table knives, dessert knives, forks and spoons, teaspoons, fish forks and knives, silver-gilt fruit knives, and silver-gilt cake forks, in addition to some 37 miscellaneous silver-gilt or silver serving pieces. It bears the mark "MC K," probably for Keller of Paris from around the beginning of the 20th century.

At a Glance

Date: c.1900
Origin: France
Brief description: A silver table service with a shaped fiddle-thread pattern, chased with foliage, mostly engraved with a crest and monogram.

Hénin & Cie Table Service
c.1890

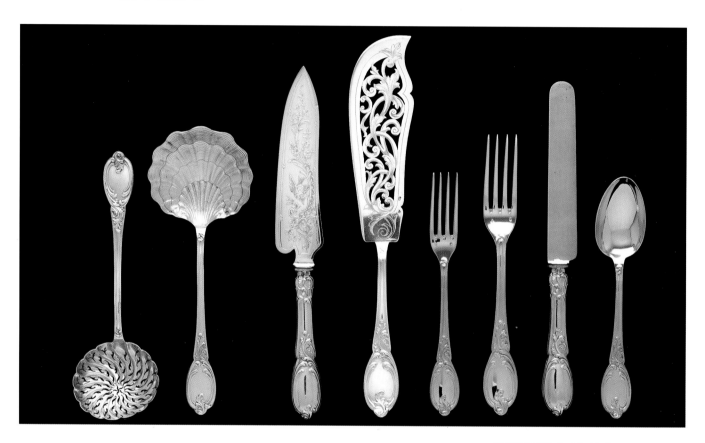

The complete service comprising some 188 pieces was the work of Hénin & Cie of Paris, a company noted for the magnificence of its flatware. The silver-gilt handles of this fine service have Rococo terminals. In addition to the usual range of dessert and table knives, forks, and spoons this service is notable for its pie forks, pastry server, stuffing spoon, sugar sifter, carving knives and forks, fish and salad servers, soup and sauce ladles, and even distinctive servers for petit fours.

At a Glance

Date: c.1890
Origin: France
Brief description: A silver-gilt and silver table service with the mark of Hénin & Cie and Rococo terminals.

Puiforcat Table Service
c.1930

The illustration shows a selection from a service of 163 pieces, accompanied by meat and entrée dishes, and a sauceboat with a detachable silver-plated liner (not shown). Unusual items in the service include asparagus tongs and separate suites of knives for butter and cheese. This remarkable service was produced in Paris by Jean Puiforcat (1897–1945) who made a brilliant debut at the Exposition des Arts Décoratifs in 1924 with stunningly dramatic geometric pieces that helped to establish the Art Deco style. By the end of the 1920s, however, he was concentrating on table services virtually devoid of ornament and with a very sleek appearance.

At a Glance

Date: c.1930
Origin: France
Brief description: A table service with the maker's mark of Puiforcat, Paris.

Jensen Flatware Service
post 1945

At a Glance

Date: Post 1945
Origin: Denmark
Brief description: A Danish silver "Acorn" pattern flatware service designed by Johan Rohde, 1915, and made by Georg Jensen.

This service of 187 pieces in sterling silver is in the acorn pattern designed about 1915 by Johan Rohde, but actually manufactured by Georg Jensen some time after World War II. This leading firm of Danish silversmiths was founded by Georg Jensen (1866–1935) who originally made his name for jewelry in the Art Nouveau idiom. About 1907, however, he joined forces with the painter Rohde (1856–1935) and together they translated the forms of post-Impressionist painting into metalwork without resorting to the facile imitation of motifs.

Kersbergen Sauce-ladles
1761

At a Glance

Date: 1761
Origin: Holland
Brief description: A pair of silver
sauce-ladles with the maker's mark of
Pieter Kersbergen, The Hague.

These sauce-ladles conform to the Old English pattern with reeded circular bowls and the mark of Pieter Kersbergen, a leading silversmith of The Hague, dating 1761. The use of the Old English pattern exemplifies the tremendous influence of English silversmiths on their European contemporaries.

Dutch Flatware Service
1921–34

At a Glance

Date: 1921–34
Origin: Holland
Brief description: A Dutch flatware service with the maker's mark C.L.J. Begeer, Utrecht, and ice server and spoons of Gerritsen & van Kempen n.v., Zeist.

Most of the 186 pieces in the complete service bear the makers' marks of C.L.J. Begeer of Utrecht (1921–34), although the ice server and matching spoons were produced by Gerritsen & van Kempen of Zeist in 1932. As well as the usual array of knives, forks, and spoons for dessert, fish, and table use it includes asparagus tongs, salad servers, custard spoons, cake slices of unusual shapes, vegetable servers, sauce ladles, a potato server, a large and two small compote servers, and two meat forks, each with pointed and thread finials.

American Flatware
1790–1848

The two tablespoons bear the marks of Tunis Dubois and Van Voorhis & Schrank, both silversmiths who flourished in New York in the late 18th century. The fish slice, on the other hand, bears the mark of the American silversmith Ford and dates from the mid 19th century. The chief interest of these items lies in their provenance as they came from the collections of silver formed or inherited by Franklin and Eleanor Roosevelt. The fish slice bears the monogram of Mary Ludlow Hall, Eleanor's grandmother, while other items in the collection bear the crest and monogram of Elizabeth Livingston Ludlow, her great-great grandmother.

At A Glance

Date: 1790–1848
Origin: USA
Brief description: A group of silver and silver-plated flatware from the private collections of Franklin and Eleanor Roosevelt and family.

American Flatware Service

20th century

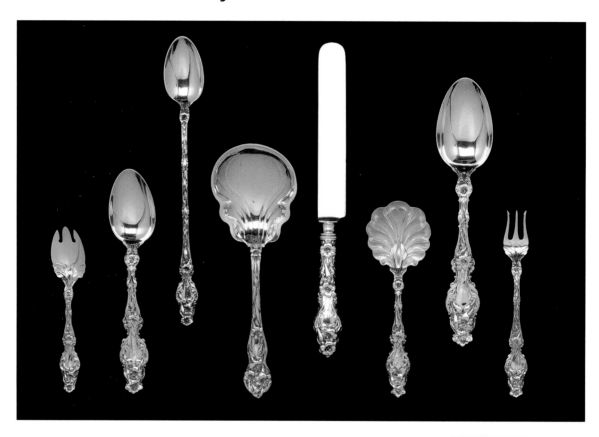

This extraordinary service, shown in part here, comprises no fewer than 347 pieces, and the knives, forks, and spoons for all occasions are in sets of 25. It includes such highly specialized items as separate suites of bouillon and demitasse spoons, ice teaspoons, salad, lunch, and seafood forks. Among the individual items are a butter serving spoon, a pierced olive spoon, a caviar spoon, a gilt pastry server, a dessert shovel, an asparagus server, and a small meat fork. The entire service was manufactured by Whiting of New York. The firm founded in 1866 by William Whiting soon absorbed its smaller rivals and produced some of the most elegant silverware of the late 19th century. It was sold to Gorham in 1924.

At A Glance

Date: 20th century
Origin: USA
Brief description: A silver flatware service by Whiting Manufacturing Company.

Tiffany Fruit Knives
1871–75

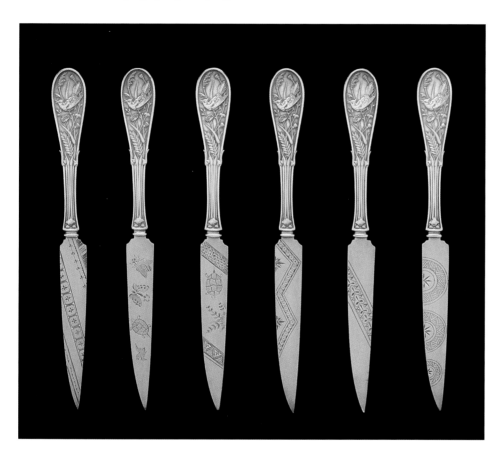

At A Glance

Date: 1871–75
Origin: USA
Brief description:
A set of six silver-gilt fruit knives marked Tiffany & Co., New York, the blades engraved with different Japanese scenes.

Because of the acid in fruit, the knives associated with it generally had steel blades, but those who preferred precious metal for both handles and blades could settle for gold-plated silver blades, and not uncommonly these were decorated as well as the handles for heightened effect. In this instance the rounded handles and pointed blades are extravagantly ornamented with Japanese scenes, insects, turtles, and geometric patterns. They were produced by Charles Louis Tiffany (1812–90) between 1871 and 1875 when the craze for all things Japanese was at its height, following the first successful penetration of Japan by Commodore Perry in 1853. Tiffany was, of course, the father of the even more celebrated Louis Comfort Tiffany, one of the foremost American exponents of the Art Nouveau style.

Child's Set

1876

At A Glance

Date: 1876
Origin: China
Brief description: A child's set consisting of knife, fork and spoon, mug, and napkin ring, all marked with Chinese characters and the maker's name K. Wong Yuen.

The flaring neck of the mug is engraved in script "Leonard Sherrell Webb Sept 23 1876 Shanghai" revealing that this enchanting service was produced for a European child, from a family in the foreign merchant community. Such Chinese wares were also exported to Europe and America. Interestingly, the cutlery has fiddle-pattern handles, showing the English influence on China.

James I Tankard
1624

At A Glance

Date: 1624
Origin: England
Brief description: A James I silver tankard, apparently lacking a maker's mark, with a tubular scroll handle, hinged flat-topped cover, and thumbpiece.

This squat lidded tankard, with slightly tapering sides and a prominent thumbpiece at the top of the tubular scroll handle, apparently lacks a maker's mark, although both body and cover bear the London assay mark for 1624, placing it in the last years of the reign of James I. Although relatively plain it is a rare piece, mainly because so much silverware was melted down to strike coins during the Civil War of 1642–49.

Charles I Flagon
1639

At A Glance

Date: 1639
Origin: England
Brief description: A Charles I silver flagon, which has a tall, slightly tapering, cylindrical body on a skirt foot, a scroll handle, a hinged, domed cover, and a bracket thumbpiece. The maker's mark is "W.C."

The difference between a tankard and a flagon is generally one of size, the former averaging between 13 and 20 ounces and the latter ranging from 20 to 40 ounces. This fine example, bearing the London assay mark of 1639, weighs 36 ounces (1,123 grams). The maker's mark "W.C." has not been identified but the body is engraved "Gilston." Remarkably this flagon remained the property of the rector and church wardens of Gilston, Essex, until they disposed of it at Sotheby's in April 1977. How it survived the commandeering of silver plate practiced by both sides in the Civil War is a miracle.

Plummer Peg Tankard
1654

At A Glance

Date: 1654
Origin: England
Brief description: A
   Commonwealth cylindrical
   peg tankard on three leaf
   and pomegranate feet with
   a fluted scroll handle, slightly
   domed cover, and double
   pomegranate thumbpiece by
   John Plummer, York.

*This interesting and unusual
vessel was manufactured by
John Plummer of York, arguably
the most important provincial
goldsmith of the
Commonwealth period. The
tankard is engraved with flowers
and foliage and the slightly
domed cover is engraved with a
coat of arms. The style of
engraving suggests Scandinavian
craftsmanship.*

Charles II Tankard
1675

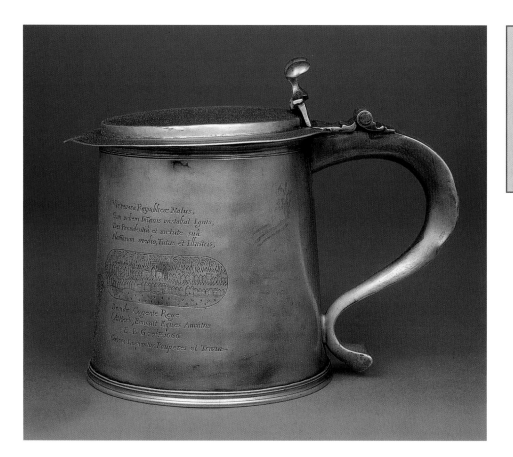

At A Glance

Date: 1675
Origin: England
Brief description: Charles II tankard engraved with scenes of the plague and the fire of London.

The royal arms of Charles II and those of Sir Edmund Berry Godfrey appear between scenes of the plague and fire of London. The tapering body sits on a molded base and the cover has a kidney thumbpiece connected to a large scroll handle. During 1665–66, Godfrey was rewarded with this gift of a tankard by the monarch for his courage and efficiency during the plague that devastated England at this time. There are several inscriptions on the tankard written in Latin, one of which reads in translation: "The gift of Sir Edmund Berry Godfrey, an active and upright magistrate who, after having rendered invaluable service in checking the progress of the plague, received from King Charles II with the consent of his Privy Council, a silver flagon to perpetuate the memory of his patriotic efforts."

George I Salver
1718

The octofoil salver by Benjamin Pyne of London was manufactured in 1718 to Britannia standard. It has eight shaped bracket feet. The Rococo cartouche enclosing the arms of Battell impaling Davies of Hope was added at a later date. The salver also bears an inscription signifying that it was purchased with a legacy from the Hon. William Maynard who died on March 7, 1716. The Britannia standard (.958 fine) was introduced in 1697 in a bid to protect the new coinage of 1696 from clipping and melting. As the coins were struck in sterling (.925 fine) silver, the higher quality now required for plate and hollowwares effectively brought the fraudulent practice of clipping to an end—although the placing of the Latin inscription Decus et Tutamen (an ornament and a safeguard) on the rim of the coins was also a pretty good deterrent to passing clipped coin.

George I Saltcellar
c.1725

At A Glance

Date: c.1725
Origin: England
Brief description: A George I silver, silver-gilt, and rock crystal saltcellar by Francis Nelme containing a Tudor silver-gilt figure of a soldier.

The celebrated Sandys Salt is a remarkable piece of great historical interest. This standing scroll saltcellar with stepped square base and canted corners supports a carved rock crystal stem enclosing a late 16th-century, silver-gilt figure of a soldier. Although the silver base and top of the saltcellar bears the mark of the London silversmith Francis Nelme, the rock crystal and gilt figurine are of Tudor origin and are believed to have descended through the Ponsonby family and passed to a kinsman, Edwin Sandys (1561–1629) whose arms are engraved upon it. Several other saltcellars incorporating silver-gilt figures dating from the period 1554–77 have also been recorded.

George III Chocolate Pot
1729

At A Glance

Date: 1729
Origin: Ireland
Brief description: A George III chocolate pot marked William Archdall, Dublin.

Chocolate was one of the new beverages that came to the British Isles after the Restoration and by the end of the 17th century distinctive pots were produced for the purpose of serving it. While ceramic chocolate pots are hard to distinguish from coffee pots of the same materials, those in silver developed quite separately, in many cases having the handle at the side, at right angles to the spout. The chief characteristic, however, is the hinged or removable finial in the domed lid through which a rod known as a molinet could be inserted to stir up the sediment without any loss of heat through opening the lid. This tapering cylindrical pot with octagonal spout and wooden scroll handle was made by William Archdall of Dublin.

George II Tea Kettle, Stand, and Lamp
1727–34

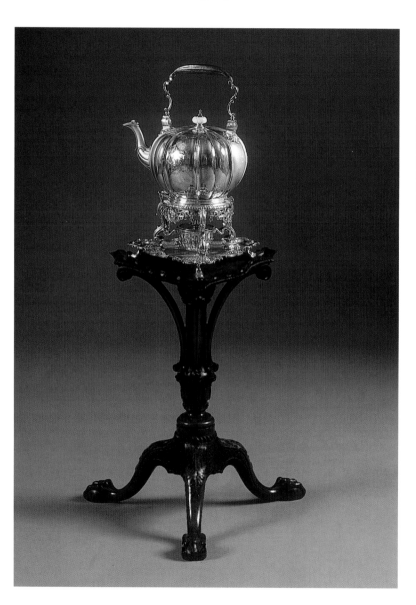

At A Glance

Date: 1727–34
Origin: England
Brief description: A George II tea kettle, stand, and lamp. The stand and kettle each engraved with a coat-of-arms within a Rococo cartouche, the lamp covered with a crest, by John White.

The triangular stand has three shell-capped dolphins' mask feet and a shell and foliage border. The kettle-stand has three shell and scroll feet and a pierced apron cast and chased with classical portrait busts. The fluted lamp has a detachable cover. The kettle is chased with broad flutes, has a covered spout, a hinged cover, and a partly leather-covered swing handle engraved with a narrow band of scalework scrolls, and foliage on a matted ground.

Selection of Tableware
1748–1909

At A Glance

Date: 1748–1909
Origin: England
Brief description: A selection of
tableware including a tea urn, coffee
pots, sauceboats, pepperettes,
saltcellars, and menu-holders.

This varied selection of tableware includes in the top row (left to right): a plated tea urn; a coffee pot, engraved with bands of bright-cut decoration; and a silver George III coffee pot by Daniel Pontifex. The center row includes a pair of George II silver saucepots by John Barbe (1748), each on three shell and scroll feet; and a pair of Edwardian pepperettes (1901), each with a detachable pierced domed cover with a bud finial. Shown in the middle is an Edwardian silver ink-blotter with a flexible base (1907). The bottom row (left to right) includes: a pair of George III silver plain boat-shaped saltcellars by John Emes (1802); a set of Edwardian menu-holders in the form of hounds' heads (1909); and a pair of George III saltcellars (1809).

Kandler Coffee Pot
c.1730

At A Glance

Date: c.1730
Origin: England
Brief description: A George II coffee pot of baluster form made by Charles Kandler. The body is divided into six panels of finely chased overlapping scallop shells between pronounced fluted ribs, the spout and handle sockets decorated to match, and completed by a carved ivory handle.

Charles Kandler was a German-born silversmith who settled in London and is regarded as the equal of Paul de Lamerie. His career was rather later (c.1727–73) and while de Lamerie began with simple Huguenot styles and then pioneered the flamboyant Rococo fashion, Kandler moved from the Rococo to simpler neo-classical forms later on.

George II Two–handled Cup and Cover
1737

At A Glance

Date: 1737
Origin: England
Brief description: A George II two-handled, baluster cup and cover with applied strapwork and later engraved foliate scrolls and lattice motifs.

Covered cups had been popular for generations, but in the early Georgian era they tended to be restricted to ceremonial purposes and their form became rather stereotyped. A typical example of this period is this baluster cup. The twin handles are capped with leaves, while the high-domed cover is decorated to match. It was produced by Louis Dupont, yet another of the craftsmen of Huguenot origins who came to England after the revocation of the Edict of Nantes in 1685, which meant that Protestants were no longer protected against persecution.

George II Porringer
1749

At A Glance

Date: 1749
Origin: England
Brief description: A George II
porringer with a circular
section body, partly fluted and
decorated with medallion
motifs by Richard Bayley.

Originally in the 17th century the porringer was a small bowl or large cup without a lid and a flat handle or tab set horizontally on one or both sides near the rim of the vessel. The word appears to be a corruption of pottager, a dish for pottage or stew. By the middle of the 18th century, porringers had become much deeper and the flat handles had been replaced by large circular handles as shown in this example made by Richard Bayley of London.

George III Tea Caddies and Sugar Box
1755

Derived from the Malay word kati, a unit of weight for tea, the original tea caddies were porcelain jars in which the precious leaves were shipped to England from the East. At a time when tea cost a pound per pound, it was a commodity that was rigorously guarded, hence the wooden case with a secure lock. Within were usually compartments for a pair of caddies, with a central mixing bowl. All three caddies here, along with the silver handle and lock on the case, bear the marks of John Swift of London.

At A Glance

Date: 1755
Origin: England
Brief description: A pair of tea caddies and matching sugar box of inverted pyriform (like flames) on circular gadrooned feet with domed covers decorated with flowers.

George III Beer Jug
1768

At A Glance

Date: 1768
Origin: England
Brief description: A George III beer jug with maker's mark of William Grundy, London.

Beer jugs with a plain bulbous or baluster body, open top, everted lid, and stout handle had been in existence since the late Middle Ages, the vast majority of the surviving examples are in pewter, which as a base alloy did not get melted down unlike silverware. As the beer jug was one of the most utilitarian vessels it was generally produced in a plain style, which did not vary much from generation to generation. This jug made by William Grundy of London in 1768 is typical, with its plain, no-nonsense baluster form on a circular foot, the only concession to ornament is the leafwork on top of the scrolled handle.

George III Condiment Vases
1781

At A Glance

Date: 1781
Origin: England
Brief description: A pair of George III condiment vases with the maker's mark of the partnership of Richard Carter, Daniel Smith, and Robert Sharp.

In an era before refrigeration, and especially at a time when it was customary to slaughter beasts before the onset of winter to minimize the costs of feeding and housing them, one of the biggest problems was dishing up meat in a palatable form. For this reason spices, pickles, and flavorings were of paramount importance, and the attention given to the preparation of condiments is reflected in the range of condiment vases and pots produced in the 17th and 18th centuries. This matching pair of tapering vases mounted on square feet have the sharply upraised handles characteristic of condiment vases and high domed covers with acorn finials.

George III Wine Coolers
1810

The fashion for white wines led to the demand for wine coolers; vessels designed to hold a single bottle with a block of ice. This pair, each on a circular molded foot, have reeded and foliage handles, gadrooned borders, and a coat-of-arms. At the top of the range are the wine coolers made of solid silver, often parcel-gilt; but on account of their size they were more usually manufactured in Sheffield plate, a technique devised by Thomas Boulsover about 1742 for fusing thin plates of silver to a copper body. In turn, it was superseded by electroplating in about 1850.

At A Glance

Date: 1810
Origin: England
Brief description: A pair of George III wine coolers manufactured by Nathan Smith & Co. of Sheffield.

George III Centerpiece
1808

At A Glance

Date: 1808
Origin: England
Brief description: A George III silver-gilt centerpiece with a triform base raised on fluted supports surmounted by three massive winged sphinxes on which rests the bowl whose undulating rim is decorated with three masks of Apollo linked with geometric Greek key bands.

The Napoleonic expedition to Egypt and the subsequent British occupation of the Lower Nile basin triggered off an insatiable interest in Pharaonic civilization. The sensational discoveries of archaeologists had a dramatic impact on all aspects of architecture and the decorative arts in the early years of the 19th century, given impetus by the lead of such connoisseurs as Thomas Hope. This centerpiece by Paul Storr is an excellent example of the rather eclectic Egyptian style, mixed with elements from classical Greece.

Regency Tankards
1815–16

A tankard of this type, made by J.W. Story and William Elliott in 1812, was included in the celebrated silver collection of HRH the "Grand Old" Duke of York, sold at Christie's after the Duke's death in 1827. Elliott made this pair a few years later. Each tankard has a tapering cylindrical body on a circular footrim, the matte surface applied with a band of infant bacchanals cavorting with goats amid fruit, drinking from a wine barrel on one and a cistern on the other.

At A Glance

Date: 1815–16
Origin: England
Brief description: A pair of Regency silver-gilt tankards with the maker's mark of William Elliott, London.

Victorian Punch Bowl
1858

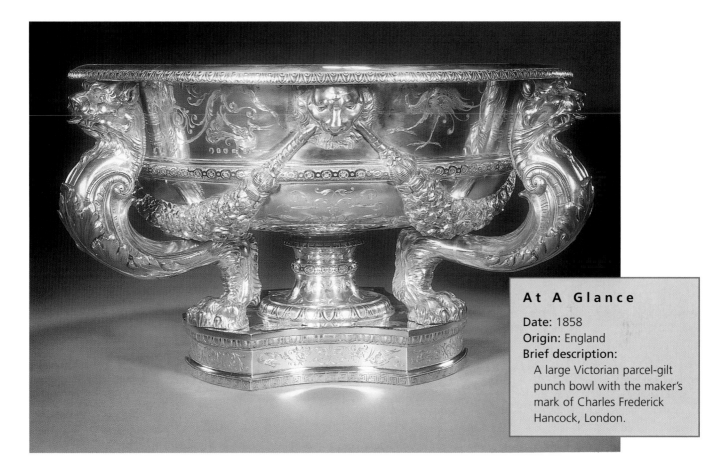

At A Glance

Date: 1858
Origin: England
Brief description:
A large Victorian parcel-gilt punch bowl with the maker's mark of Charles Frederick Hancock, London.

Punch, a word derived from the Hindu number five, was a beverage which combined wines or spirits with sugar, spices, fruit, and water. As its name suggests, it was imported from India in the late 17th century and inevitably inspired large vessels, often with pronounced scalloped rims. This example was produced by Charles Frederick Hancock of Bruton Street, London, one of the most fashionable silversmiths of the mid-Victorian period. The circular bowl is on a shaped triangular base, with a central baluster support and three leaf-capped lion-monopodia bracket supports with three lion masks and floral swags between. The base and bowl are engraved with grotesque birds, harpies, and demi-figures in the Renaissance style.

67

Victorian Jug
1868–99

At A Glance

Date: 1868–99
Origin: England
Brief description: A Victorian jug with a slender, tapering neck, engraved with stiff leaf ornament and raised on a similar foot. It has the maker's mark of George Fox.

The most interesting feature of this silver jug is the reeded handle attached to the body that has a grotesque mask and terminates in an acanthus and anthemion motif. The interior of the jug has been gilded to protect it from the corrosive acids in fruit juice.

Victorian Two-handled Vase
1877

At A Glance

Date: 1877
Origin: Scotland
Brief description: A Victorian two-handled vase with the maker's mark of Marshall & Sons, Edinburgh.

In 1771 the fragments of a huge vase were discovered at Tivoli near Rome and came into the possession of the British ambassador to Naples, Sir William Hamilton, who had the vase repaired before presenting it to his nephew George, second Earl of Warwick. It was later purchased by Sir William Burrell and is now one of the gems in the Burrell Collection, Glasgow. It inspired reduced-size replicas in ceramics as well as silver. This example was produced by Marshall & Sons of Edinburgh in 1877.

Entrée Dishes and Flagon 1868–83

At A Glance

Date: 1868–83
Origin: England
Brief description: A set of four Victorian entrée dishes, covers, stands, and lamps of 1883 by Robert Garrard, and a flagon of 1868 by Daniel and Charles Houle, London.

The octagonal entrée dishes by Robert Garrard (1883) have tented covers and matching stands on four leaf-capped shell and scroll feet. This firm was one of the largest and most fashionable for much of the 19th century and survives to this day, having been the Crown Jewellers since 1843. In the Victorian era it was noted for its extravagant exhibition pieces, although it was also renowned for its flatware and fine domestic hollowwares. The flagon by Daniel and Charles Houle of London (1869) has a hinged domed cover and foliage thumbpiece.

Dresser Claret Jug
1882

At A Glance

Date: 1882
Origin: England
Brief description: A late-Victorian claret jug designed by Christopher Dresser and made by Roberts of Sheffield.

The chief interest of this silver claret jug by Roberts of Sheffield, modeled in the style of a late-medieval flagon, is the fact that it was designed by Christopher Dresser (1834–1904), an exact contemporary of William Morris. Although he spent two years at the Somerset House School of Design, Dr Dresser became a university lecturer and botanist. Later he combined his botanical studies with his early design training to revolutionize the late-Victorian approach to the applied arts in ceramics, glass, and furniture as well as silver.

Edwardian Irish Presentation Cup
1909

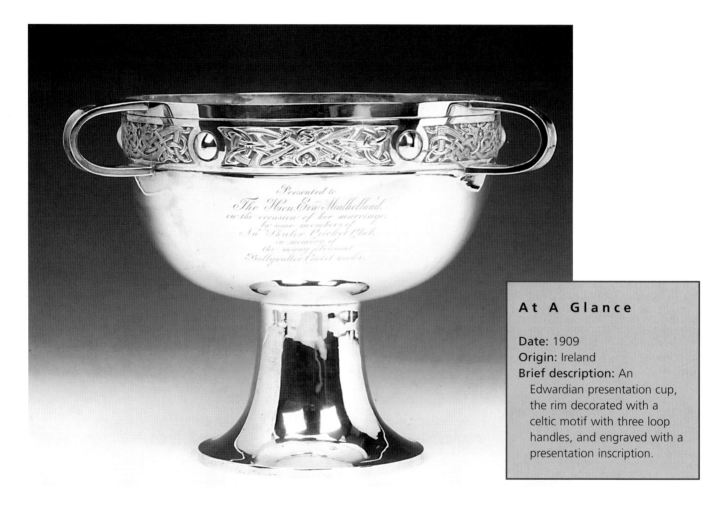

At A Glance

Date: 1909
Origin: Ireland
Brief description: An
Edwardian presentation cup,
the rim decorated with a
celtic motif with three loop
handles, and engraved with a
presentation inscription.

From the late-Victorian period onward large silver was virtually confined to prize trophies and presentation pieces, and the personal inscriptions engraved on them add considerably to their interest. This large cup manufactured at Dublin has a circular bowl raised on a trumpet foot and the rim is decorated with the Hiberno-Norse ring-chain motif and three applied loop handles. The engraved inscription related to a presentation made to the Hon. Eva Mulholland by members of the Na Shuber Cricket Club.

Guild of Handicrafts Cruet Set
1912

At A Glance

Date: 1912
Origin: England
Brief description:
A Guild of Handicrafts cruet set comprising: pedestal salt with green glass liner, pepper, mustard pot and cover with green glass liner, and two small serving spoons, all with a hammered finish.

The chemical properties of sodium chloride (common salt) posed problems for silversmiths and for that reason the pedestal salt (on the left of the picture) has a liner of green glass to prevent the salt coming in contact with the silver. There was no such problem with pepper or other spices, so the pot in the center was entirely made of silver. On the right stands a matching mustard pot with a flat-domed lid and a similar green glass liner. The suite is completed by a pair of tiny spoons. This set was manufactured by the Guild of Handicrafts workshop in London.

Edward & Sons Tea and Coffee Service 1926

Although the 1920s was a decade that witnessed exciting developments in the applied and decorative arts, such as the transition from Art Nouveau to Art Deco and Art Moderne, and the influence of the Bauhaus, there was still a tremendous demand for silverware in traditional patterns. This service by Edward & Sons of Glasgow, comprising tea and coffee pots with cream jug and sugar bowl, is firmly in the Georgian tradition.

At A Glance

Date: 1926
Origin: Scotland
Brief description: A four-piece tea and coffee service in simple oval forms on four trefoil-headed paw feet and shaped scrolled rims and handles.

Omar Ramsden Tea Caddy
1926

At A Glance

Date: 1926
Origin: England
Brief description: An octagonal tea caddy with a central Tudor rose on its slightly domed cover by Omar Ramsden.

After the globular or cylindrical caddies of the 18th century, housed in locked cabinets, there developed a fashion for individual caddies of square, rectangular, or polygonal forms, and these styles have predominated to the present time. This octagonal hand-hammered caddy on a stepped foot with a slightly domed cover terminating in a central Tudor rose is inscribed in Latin "Omar Ramsden me fecit, London 1926." Omar Ramsden (1873–1939) was born in Sheffield, but settled in London in 1898 where he established his studio in collaboration with the silversmith Alwynn Carr. They parted company in 1918 and in the ensuing period Ramsden turned from Celtic styles to the Art Deco pieces on which his reputation now rests.

Crichton Beer Jug
1934

At A Glance

Date: 1934
Origin: England
Brief description:
   A modern silver beer jug with maker's mark of L.A. Crichton.

This pear-shaped jug by L.A. Crichton is raised on a spreading foot, with a beak-form spout and a scroll handle. It has the timeless quality of good silver and decorative features have been kept to a bare minimum; the function of the beer jug dictates the form.

Austrian Compotes
late 19th century

This type of dish takes its name from the French term for fruit cooked in syrup and then served cold. Such dishes are invariably constructed with a shallow bowl on a tall stem. In this case, the pair of compotes have stems in the shape of fluted inverted pears, mounted on fluted circular bases. The bowl is of a campana form, with lobed and compressed sides, flaring border and applied reeded wavy rims. Unfortunately no maker's mark is discernible on either dish, which detracts from their value to the collector.

At A Glance

Date: Late 19th century
Origin: Austria
Brief description: A pair of compotes with stems in the shape of fluted inverted pears, mounted on fluted circular bases, and campana bowls.

German Turbo Shell Cup
1630

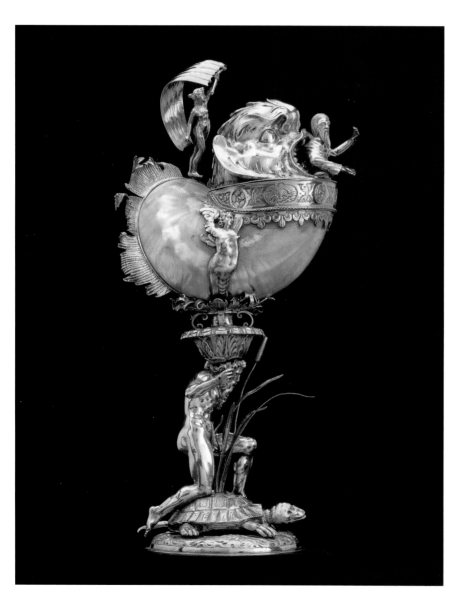

At A Glance

Date: 1630
Origin: Germany
Brief description: A parcel-gilt turbo shell cup and cover possibly by one of the Meyer family of silversmiths.

This extraordinary vessel in the shape of a turban or turbo shell stands on a raised circular base chased with sea monsters among the waves. It is surmounted by a detachable cast model of a turtle while the stem forms the kneeling figure of Neptune. The shell itself encloses two winged female caryatids surmounted by a figure of Venus Fortuna, the border chased with a band of sea monsters. Vessels of this type are sometimes referred to as nautilus cups and this example was produced at Ulm, possibly by one of the Meyer family of silversmiths.

Rohde Charger
1688–1717

At A Glance

Date: 1688–1717
Origin: Germany
Brief description:
A large silver charger made by Peter Rohde III.

Large silver dishes of this type were intended for special occasions and were decorated to suit the occasion. In this instance the shaped, circular, embossed, and chased dish is ornamented with a classical scene showing the departure of Briseis from Troy (alluded to in Homer's Iliad). The everted border is chased with scrolls and leafy motifs with a reeded rim. It was created by Peter Rohde III, one of a distinguished family of silversmiths who resided in Danzig, East Prussia (now known as Gdansk in Poland).

Knuysting Cruet Set
1796

At A Glance

Date: 1796
Origin: Netherlands
Brief description: A silver-gilt
cruet frame containing two
cut-glass bottles and stoppers, and a set of four salts.

The cruet frame contains two cut-glass bottles and stoppers for oil and vinegar, the stand itself being boat-shaped with a pierced gallery and scroll foliate handles. Like the salts, with their blue-glass liners, the cruet was made in the Louis XIV style by Cornelis Knuysting of Rotterdam (1730–1812). He was a prolific silversmith who produced table services and flatware. He worked with his son-in-law Jan George Grebe who carried on the business after Knuysting's death.

Jensen Table Lighter
early 20th century

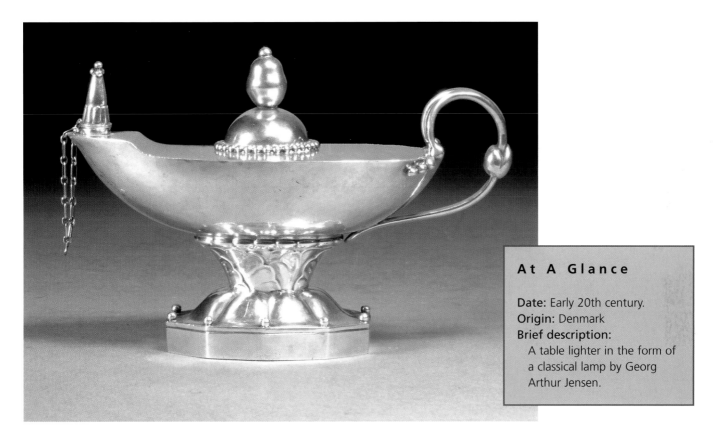

At A Glance

Date: Early 20th century.
Origin: Denmark
Brief description:
   A table lighter in the form of
   a classical lamp by Georg
   Arthur Jensen.

This is an excellent example of a classical subject revived for a completely different purpose. Superficially it resembles an Etruscan oil lamp, complete with conical snuffer and chain, but in reality it is a table lighter for cigars. It was made in the early 20th century by Georg Arthur Jensen (1866–1935). Trained as a sculptor, Jensen opened his own workshop in Copenhagen in 1904, primarily making jewelry, but three years later he teamed up with the architect and painter Johan Rohde and the silversmith Harald Nielsen and quickly established a reputation for good-quality silverware.

Rohde Tea and Coffee Service
post 1945

At A Glance

Date: Post 1945
Origin: Denmark
Brief description: A four-piece tea and coffee service on a two-handled tray designed by Johan Rohde and made by Georg Jensen Silversmithy.

Designed by Johan Rohde, this Cosmos pattern service was executed by Georg Jensen Silversmithy after World War II. It comprises a teapot, slightly baluster coffee pot, sugar bowl, and cream jug, each with subtle hammered finish, the lower body chased with vertical fronds. The pots have partly reeded carved wood and silver handles with trifurcated scroll and beaded join. The detachable lids have a fluted calyx design rising to partly fluted ball finials.

Danish Biscuit Box
post 1945

At A Glance

Date: Post 1945
Origin: Denmark
Brief description: A silver biscuit box designed by Harald Nielsen and made by Georg Jensen Silversmithy.

The biscuit box is marked pattern 440 and the plain cylindrical body has a slightly rounded rim with a circular foot. The detachable cover has a slight rise in the center and a finial of beads and leaves capped by a large ball. Wares of this type epitomize the best of Scandinavian silver in the post-war period.

Ornamental French Vases
19th century

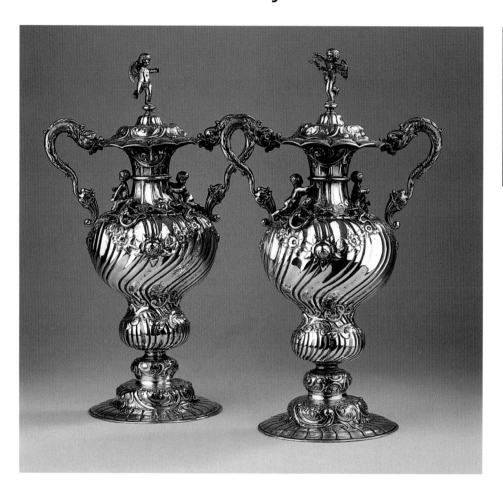

At A Glance

Date: 19th century
Origin: France
Brief description: Two ornamental vases with matching
   covers with indistinct marks.

Although very similar these silver vases are not actually a pair, and the fact that the makers' marks are illegible makes correct attribution impossible, a fact which tends to detract from their value. Nevertheless, the workmanship is of a very high order and it is probable that they were produced by the same silversmith. Each vase has a circular fluted base rising to a knobbed stem chased with scrolls and flowers. The fluted body is similarly decorated, with two putti (cherubs) and six reptiles attached to the neck. The handles are in the form of dolphins, while the domed cover in each case is surmounted with a putto.

Continental Nef
19th century

At A Glance

Date: 19th century
Origin: Portugal
Brief description:
A silver and silver-gilt nef with the maker's mark of Gaspar Vieira.

The word nef appears to be derived ultimately from the Latin navis, *meaning a ship. Models of fully-rigged galleons developed in the late Middle Ages as centerpieces which also served the useful purposes of a salt container or sometimes a vessel for the bottle of wine reserved for the host or an honored guest. The concept was revived in the 19th century and used as a medium to demonstrate the versatility of the silversmith, not only in the delicacy of the rigging and the sails but also in such features as miniature cannon. Nefs of this period were often decorated in enamels and set with precious or semi-precious stones. This example was produced by Gaspar Vieira of Lisbon, Portugal.*

Auroc *surtout de table*
c.1890

At A Glance

Date: c.1890
Origin: France
Brief description: An impressive *surtout de table* with the maker's mark of André Auroc.

Although in the 18th century style, this remarkable centerpiece is very much a product of the 19th century in its sumptuousness and eclecticism. The shaped quatrefoil plateau rests on four scroll and plinth feet, each surmounted by a mask with scroll, husk, and plinth branch. The wax pan is gadrooned and surmouted by a vase-shaped socket. The whole is replete with applied rock, shell, and scroll cartouches, the center engraved with classical portrait busts, birds, flowers, and foliage. This extravaganza was created by André Auroc of Paris for Prince Murat, inspired by a famous centerpiece which had been made by Claude Ballin of Paris in the 1720s for the Tsar of Russia.

English Nef
1911

At A Glance

Date: 1911
Origin: England
Brief description: A large
silver nef with sponsor's mark
of D. and J. Wellby, London.

This example is formed as a three-masted ship mounted on four openwork wheels. The hull is chased with winged putti, mermaids, mermen, and grotesque monsters. The figurehead is an eagle and the hinged rudder is ornately chased. The sides of the vessel have applied coats of arms and lions' masks, while the deck is covered with numerous sailors and cannon. Despite some pseudo-French marks, this nef was retailed by D. and J. Welby of London who may have imported it from the Continent.

Art Nouveau Fruit Stand
early 20th century

At A Glance

Date: Early 20th century.
Origin: England
Brief description:
A silvered brass and glass fruit stand with the maker's mark "WMF."

As this piece is essentially made of base metal it does not bear the hallmarks associated with silverware, although there is the maker's mark "WMF." It is not untypical of many large pieces in the last years of the 19th century and early years of the 20th century where cheaper alternatives to precious metal were considered perfectly in tune with the spirit of Art Nouveau. This is a splendid example of the genre, with the glass liner held by sprays of maple leaves, and the quadripartite stand and feet cast in the form of plant stalks with foliage at the base.

Cardeilhac Soup Tureen
late 19th century

At A Glance

Date: Late 19th century.
Origin: France
Brief description: A covered soup tureen and matching stand with the maker's mark of Cardeilhac, Paris.

The octagonal spreading stand has molded borders and supports the tureen which has fluted borders and scroll bracket handles. The detachable domed cover has a detachable artichoke finial. Both stand and tureen are chased with a band of shells, scrolls, and diaperwork. They were the work of Ernest Cardeilhac who produced jewelry and silverware in the best traditions of Art Nouveau, eschewing the more bizarre fantasies of the style and concentrating on good, sober designs which were eminently saleable in the 1890s. Cardeilhac died in 1904 but his sons James and Peter carried on the family tradition until 1951 when the firm amalgamated with Christophle.

Odiot and Puiforcat Service
c.1900

At A Glance

Date: c.1900
Origin: France
Brief description: A silver and silver-plated seven-piece tea and coffee service by Odiot, and rectangular trays by Emile Puiforcat, a set of dishes, and a serving dish and cover.

This interesting service comprises teapot, coffee pot, samovar, sugar bowl, and cream jug manufactured by Odiot of Paris, with circular and rectangular trays by Emile Puiforcat of Paris. The vessels are uniformly decorated with foliage, shells, and scrolls. Although the product of two different silversmiths the service is engraved with the monogram "MF," presumably the original owner. It is accompanied by a set of dishes and a twin-handled serving dish with matching cover.

Puiforcat Tea and Coffee Service
c.1940

At A Glance

Date: c.1940
Origin: France
Brief description:
   A four-piece tea and coffee service comprising teapot, coffee pot, covered sugar bowl, and cream jug by Jean E. Puiforcat.

Emile Puiforcat was succeeded by his even more famous son Jean (1897–1945) who trained in the family firm and produced some excellent hollowwares in the Art Nouveau idiom before adopting the more angular styles of the 1920s. At the Exposition des Arts Décoratifs in Paris, 1925, he stole the show with an astounding range of silver which helped establish the Art Deco fashion. He continued to produce elegant hollowwares and services in this style until his death at the end of World War II. This service, comprising teapot, coffee pot, covered sugar bowl, and cream jug is characterized by a partly spreading cylindrical form with reeded rim bases and collars or rims of similar pattern.

Christophle Coffee Pot and Sugar Bowl c.1940

As a rule silver-plate is not much reckoned by collectors, but when it is the product of one of the outstanding designers, they are prepared to make an exception. This silver-plated coffee pot is severely functional in appearance and devoid of ornamentation, but the cinnamon-colored lacquer handle and its unusual mounting reveal something out of the ordinary. With its matching sugar bowl, it has a lightly reeded trim. Both were produced by Christophle, a Parisian firm founded by Charles Christophle in 1839, best remembered for pioneering electroplate in France in 1861.

At A Glance

Date: c.1940
Origin: France
Brief description: A silver-plated coffee pot with lacquer handle and a matching sugar bowl by Christophle.

Italian Soup Tureen
1787

At A Glance

Date: 1787
Origin: Italy
Brief description:
An important soup tureen, cover, and stand, the property of a Genoese noble family.

The circular stand, on four acanthus foliage-capped ball feet, has a border chased with a band of waterleaves. The two-handled tureen has a chased border of foliage, the lower part of the fluted body chased with palm leaves and the upper part with Vitruvian scrolls and flowers on a matted ground. The whole ensemble, made in Genoa, shows the marked influence of the French architect Charles de Wailly who was working at the Palazzo Spinola at this time.

Buccellatti Vases
late 20th century

At A Glance

Date: Late 20th century
Origin: Italy
Brief description:
A large pair of cylindrical vases with an all-over matte finish, by Buccellatti.

Each of these vases has a bulbous cylindrical body, with a lobed, out-turned upper border. The surface has an over-all fine matte finish, applied on the sides with four tapering panels of overlapping acanthus leaves. They were produced by the firm of Buccellatti, which, originating in Italy, now has branches in the United States as well. It was founded by Mario Buccellatti (born 1891) who established his own business in 1919. The firm's trademark includes the slogan "Maestro Paragon Coppella," meaning "master of precious metals," an epithet first applied by Mario's most famous customer of the 1920s, the poet Gabriele d'Annunzio.

Baskakov Tea Caddy and Sugar Box
c.1910

At A Glance

Date: c.1910
Origin: Russia
Brief description: A tea caddy and matching sugar box with the maker's mark of Petr Baskakov, Moscow.

Both pieces are in the form of a cube with a domed top, engraved with stylized flowers and depicting a Chinaman on one side. The sugar box has a hinged cover and is silver-gilt inside, while the caddy has a detachable cap and stopper. These items were produced by Petr Baskakov of Moscow who flourished between 1908 and the revolution. The decoration reveals the profound influence of Jugendstil, the German version of Art Nouveau.

Fabergé Silver-mounted Glass Bottle
c.1890

At A Glance

Date: c.1890
Origin: Russia
Brief description: A silver-mounted glass bottle with the maker's mark of Julius Rappaport, workmaster for Peter Carl Fabergé.

The smokey glass body is oblong in shape and is decorated with an engraved silver mount suspending garlands, while the circular lobed cap has similar festoons over a fluted case. The slightly domed top has a pellet finial. It bears the marks of Julius Rappaport, workmaster for Peter Carl Fabergé (1846–1920), the most distinguished Russian silversmith of his generation. Although best remembered for the sumptuously jeweled Easter eggs created for the Imperial Family, Fabergé also produced a very wide range of hollowwares.

Fabergé Punch Service
c.1910

The large cut-glass silver covered bowl has large silver circular bands with stylized flowerheads and foliage within beaded and reeded rims and rests on a circular stand with reeded handles and paw feet. It is accompanied by 24 cut-glass silver-mounted goblets and a silver ladle. The rim of the bowl has the Fabergé mark with the Imperial warrant of 1908–17, but the marks on the other pieces are false. Nevertheless this service is a fine example of Russian silver just before the revolution.

At A Glance

Date: c.1910
Origin: Russia
Brief description: A cut-glass punch bowl with silver circular bands on a tray, mounted goblets, and a ladle.

Swedish Decanters and Candlesticks 1920

At A Glance

Date: 1920
Origin: Sweden
Brief description: A pair of cut-glass silver-mounted decanters decorated with trophies and birds and a pair of small candlesticks by W.A. Bolin, Stockholm.

The decanters stand on a raised base decorated with trophies and birds, while the cut-glass baluster bodies are applied with silver roses, foliage, and fruit baskets. The scroll handles are attached to hinged covers with cupid finials among grapes. The two candlesticks are of a fairly traditional design. These items were produced by W.A. Bolin of Stockholm who held the position of crown jewelers to the Swedish monarchy.

American Compote
c.1865

At A Glance

Date: c.1865
Origin: USA
Brief description: A medallion-pattern compote by Ball, Black & Company (succeeded by Black, Starr & Frost in 1874).

The circular spreading foot supports a stem with applied medallions at the knop. The oval two-handled body has a chased border of grape leaves and a beaded border, with two realistically modeled rams heads applied to each side. The handles are decorated with cherubic masks. This compote was produced by the New York firm of Ball, Black & Company which traced its origins back to 1810 but which came to prominence in the 1850s, before changing its name to Black, Starr and Frost in 1876.

American Butter Pats
1877–78

Each has a finely frosted finish with Oriental motifs which include a blue jay, a dragon, a bird in flight, a butterfly, and a fan with geometric bands. The firm which produced this set was founded by Jabez Gorham at Providence, Rhode Island, in 1831 but eventually had branches in many parts of the USA and has been responsible for a prodigious output of decorative and useful wares ever since.

At A Glance

Date: 1877–78
Origin: USA.
Brief description: A set of five parcel-gilt butter pats made by Gorham Manufacturing Company.

Tiffany Ewers
1873–91

At A Glance

Date: 1873–91
Origin: USA
Brief description: A pair of large silver ewers decorated with foliage, dancing putti, and satyrs, by Tiffany & Co., New York.

Each has a vase form on a waisted square base, the body chased with bands of acanthus leaves and grapevines between a frieze of dancing putti and satyrs. The spiral fluted neck is applied with a bacchanalian mask, while the angular handle terminates in acanthus rosettes. These ewers were produced by Tiffany of New York, the most prestigious name in the history of the applied and decorative arts in America. Founded by Charles Lewis Tiffany (1812–1902) in 1834, it excelled in all branches, not the least in its elegant silver wares.

American Egg Boiler and Clock
1895

At A Glance

Date: 1895
Origin: USA
Brief description: A Gale &
  Willis egg boiler and
  matching clock given by
  Mrs. Valentine G. Hall,
  Eleanor Roosevelt's great
  grandmother, as a wed-
  ding gift to Eleanor and
  Franklin Roosevelt.

The egg boiler is triangular in section and is fitted with three egg-holders and surmounted by an hour glass. The sides are decorated with engine-turning, engraved with village scenes, and it comes with a detachable burner stand. Like the little clock, produced by Gale & Willis of New York, it was a wedding present to Eleanor and Franklin Delano Roosevelt. Both are fully described in the wedding present book on display at the Franklin D. Roosevelt Library, Hyde Park, New York.

American Presentation Cup
1898

At A Glance

Date: 1898
Origin: USA
Brief description: A three-handled presentation cup given as a gift from Admiral Dewey to Admiral Richmond P. Hobson.

The cup is in the form of an urn. There is a swirling base and a female figure holds aloft a wreath and a scroll inscribed "DEWEY," while a female winged figure rises above. Engravings of poetry include a long inscription from the Piccadilly Club of Cincinnati to Admiral Dewey in celebration of his defeat of the enemy at Manila during the Spanish-American War. Dewey, in turn, presented it to Admiral Richmond P. Hobson, commander of the Merrimac during that campaign.

DeMatteo Tea and Coffee Service c.1950

At A Glance

Date: c.1950
Origin: USA.
Brief description: A four-piece tea and coffee service comprising: coffee pot, teapot, cream jug, and covered sugar bowl, by William G. DeMatteo, New York.

The design of the service is all in a globular form supported on three fluted feet. The hinged domed covers have applied blossom finials while the handles are of fluted ivory. The service stands on a tray with two openwork blossom handles. It was manufactured by William G. DeMatteo of New York.

Persian Dinner Service
19th century

At A Glance

Date: 19th century
Origin: Persia (Iran)
Brief description: A selection of Eastern silver including Persian silver cups and saucers, incised with animals among flowers and foliage, and small boxes.

A considerable amount of silver was brought back to Britain from India, Afghanistan, and Persia in the 19th century, partly as booty in innumerable campaigns and wars, but latterly through legitimate trade in the souks and bazaars of the east. It must be admitted that much of it is inferior in quality and stereotyped in design but pieces of fine appearance and excellent workmanship do exist and attract the keen attention of the discerning collector. In more recent years a lot of Oriental silver has been repatriated as indigenous demand develops for the best 19th-century wares.

Oriental Rosewater Ewer and Basin
late 19th century

At A Glance

Date: Late 19th century
Origin: Near East
Brief description: A rosewater ewer and basin, probably Turkish, of fluted baluster form.

This is Oriental silver at its best; both vessels are of a fluted design and the ewer in particular is of a very elegant baluster appearance. The basin has a pierced central boss and screw for securing to the pot. Silver of this type, despite its quality, is seldom marked. The ewer and basin are definitely of Near Eastern origin and are probably Turkish.

Middle Eastern Vases
20th century

At A Glance

Date: 20th century
Origin: Middle East
Brief description: A pair of
vases decorated in relief.

Both vessels have an ovoid shape and are lavishly decorated in relief with a multitude of fish cavorting amid the foaming waves. The signatures on their bases are indistinct and some research into this would probably enhance their value at auction.

Charles II and William III Candlesticks 1682–99

The pair of Charles II candlesticks (left) have the maker's mark "AH," 1682, each on a stepped square base with fluted column rising from a square knop, with a plain square socket and detachable nozzle with pricket. The pair of William III candlesticks (right) by William Denny and John Bache were made in 1699 to Britannia standard. Each stands on a square base with cut corners and fluted column, reeded socket, and square nozzle with gadrooned borders.

At A Glance

Date: 1682–99
Origin: England
Brief description: A pair of Charles II candlesticks (left) with maker's mark "AH," 1682, and a pair of William III candlesticks (right) by William Denny and John Bache, London, 1699.

George I Candlesticks
1720

They stand on shaped square bases with sunken centres, while the partly octagonal baluster stems are surmounted by vase-shaped sockets. They have the maker's mark of Samuel Margas overstriking that of Anthony Nelme, 1720. Nelme, a London silversmith of Huguenot origin, flourished at the end of the 17th century and the business was continued after his death in 1722 by his son Francis. He also produced teapots and pilgrim bottles but is chiefly remembered for his candlesticks.

Paul de Lamerie Candlesticks
1719

Each candlestick is on a stepped square-shaped base with incurved angles, while the slender octagonal baluster stems have spool-shaped sockets. They reflect de Lamerie's early style, as they are virtually devoid of ornament relying instead on their elegant lines for their appeal.

At A Glance

Date: 1719
Origin: England
Brief description: A pair of George I candlesticks by Paul de Lamerie made to Britannia standard.

Early Georgian Candlesticks
1738–47

The first pair (left) was made by George Wickes in 1738. Each has a square-shaped base with baluster stem and spool-shaped socket and detachable nozzle. The other pair of candlesticks (right) was produced by Edward Wakelin in 1747. Both pairs are engraved with the arms of the Roundell family of Yorkshire. George Wickes was one of the most prominent London silversmiths in the period from 1735 to 1747 and his shop in Panton Street was patronized by many noblemen including Frederick, Prince of Wales. Edward Wakelin, operating at a slightly later period, also had many of the aristocracy and the royal family among his clients.

George II Candlesticks
c.1745

These matching candlesticks bear the mark of Peter Archambo working in London about 1745, but lacking a hallmark. Each has a triangular base with spirally fluted column, Corinthian capital socket and detachable square-shaped nozzle. The Rococo bases are cast and chased with shells, scrolls, and flowers. Archambo, another of the silversmiths of French Huguenot descent, seems to have worked closely with Wickes and Wakelin, supplying them with articles to complete services as well as operating on his own account.

At A Glance

Date: c.1745
Origin: England
Brief description: A set of four matching, George II candlesticks with the maker's mark of Peter Archambo, but no hallmark.

George III Candlesticks
1775

At A Glance

Date: 1775
Origin: England
Brief description: A pair of rare George III silver-gilt candlesticks by John Parker and Edward Wakelin.

These sticks in the Louis XVI "antique style" were manufactured in 1775 by John Parker and Edward Wakelin, partners and successors to George Wickes who were noted for fine silverware that was strongly influenced by French forms. Each has a circular, slightly spreading base with reed-and-tie border and a baluster stem formed as three female herms hung with drapery and berried foliage. The base has three crests in cartouches, while there are two crests on the nozzle.

George IV Three-light Candelabra
1821

At A Glance

Date: 1821
Origin: England
Brief description: A pair of George III silver-gilt, three-light candelabra in the antique style with the maker's mark of Philip Rundell.

Each candlestick has a spreading circular base with a shell and gadrooned border. The stems are decorated with acanthus foliage and have two detachable acanthus leaf-capped scroll branches with acanthus flower decoration. At the top, detachable sockets are in the shape of Roman lamps with detachable shaped circular nozzles. The bases are applied twice with a coat-of-arms, and the sockets and nozzles are each engraved with two crests.

Louis XV Candlesticks
1719

At A Glance

Date: 1719
Origin: France
Brief description: A pair of Louis XV silver candlesticks with baluster stems and spool-shaped sockets.

These elegant candlesticks bear the maker's mark of Antoine Filassier who flourished in Paris at the beginning of the 18th century. They date from 1719, early in the long reign of Louis XV, and exhibit the restraint in decoration and form which characterized the period before Rococo style took over. Each candlestick has a large circular, spreading foot, with a slender baluster stem and spool-shaped socket. The base is decorated with strapwork and a husk border on a matted ground, the socket being similarly ornamented. Decoration on the stem is restricted to a guilloche border and husk and rosette flutes. Both bases are engraved with a coat of arms surmounted by the coronet of a marquess.

Louis XV Lenhendrick Candlesticks 1768–73

At A Glance

Date: 1768 and 1773
Origin: France
Brief description: A pair of Louis XV silver candlesticks with baluster stems, vase sockets, and Rococo decoration.

Louis XV came to the throne in 1715 at the age of five, succeeding his great-grandfather, Louis XIV. His reign of almost 60 years coincided with the great age of decorative art, dominated by the Rococo style which is often regarded as synonymous with Louis Quinze, although this extravagant style reached its zenith in the closing years of this reign. Although dated five years apart, both of these candlesticks were designed and manufactured by the same silversmith, Louis-Joseph Lenhendrick. Each is on a shaped circular base with elaborate baluster stem, vase-shaped socket, and detachable shaped circular nozzle. The bases are cast and chased with shells, foliate scrolls, and husks while the stems are fluted and chased with trailing acanthus foliage and flower garlands.

Louis XV Candlesticks
1745

At A Glance

Date: 1745
Origin: France
Brief description: A pair of Louis XV candlesticks with the maker's mark of Alexis Loir, Paris.

These candlesticks were made by Alexis Loir of Paris and are believed to be the pair which was formerly in the Puiforcat Collection. They stand on shaped circular stepped bases with dentilated and reed and trefoil bands, rising to fluted tapering and knopped stems, headed by octagonal shoulders. The circular campana-shaped sockets have removable reeded and shell nozzles.

Louis XVI Candlesticks
1789

At A Glance

Date: 1789
Origin: France
Brief description: A pair of Louis XVI candlesticks with the maker's mark of Henri Auguste and engraved with the arms of the Prince of Wales, later King George IV.

These candlesticks have a spreading circular base with a tapering cylindrical stem, spool-shaped sockets and detachable nozzles, chased and applied with bands of beading, laurel leaves, anthemion ornament, and flutes. They bear the crest of the Prince of Wales (later King George IV) and were made by Henri Auguste. He was a fashionable Parisian silversmith, who created these on the eve of the revolution, which put a drastic, if temporary, stop to the production of fine wares.

Candelabra and Soup Tureen
late 19th century

The silver-plated candelabra have circular bases decorated with beading, while the knopped stems rise to support three branches terminating in sockets with flared rims. They are matched by a large, deep tureen from the same manufacturer and decorated in the same manner.

The escalating cost of silver drove manufacturers to seek cheaper substitutes. From 1742 Sheffield plate, involving the fusing of a thin sheet of silver to a copper body, was a tolerable substitute, but George Elkington of Birmingham pioneered electroplating in 1843 which within a few years was being widely used to deposit a thin layer of silver on a copper or bronze body as well as replacing the traditional methods of gilding silver itself.

At A Glance

Date: Late 19th century
Origin: Italy
Brief description: A pair of silver-plated candelabra, flanking a soup tureen.

Hoffman Tray and Candlesticks 1907

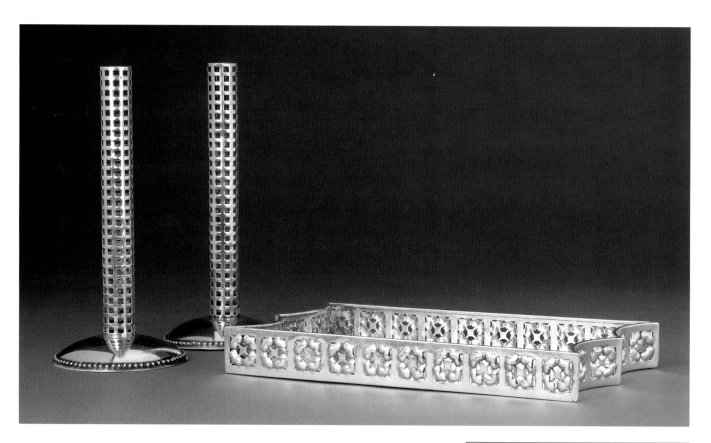

The candlesticks have broad, flat circular bases of a severely plain form while the stems are slender cylinders with rectangular fretting and plain tops. They are matched by a rectangular tray with indented sides and a pierced border. Both tray and candlesticks were designed by Josef Hoffman (1870–1955) and executed by craftsmen of the Wiener Werkstätte, which he helped to found in June 1903. His cubist designs for hollowware and furniture astounded the public but had an enormous influence on the development of the applied arts in Europe.

At A Glance

Date: 1907
Origin: Austria
Brief description: A silver tray and matching pair of candlesticks designed by Joself Hoffman and made by the Wiener Werkstätte.

Dutch Wall Sconces
1688

At A Glance

Date: 1688
Origin: Holland
Brief description: A pair of wall
sconces in the shape of scrolled
branches decorated with leaves and
fruit.

Wall sconces were brackets designed for
candles or rush lights and they were
often produced in pairs or matched sets.
Originally of cast or wrought iron by
the late 16th century they were
emerging in silver and were regarded as
status symbols. The plain forms gave
way in the 17th century to very
elaborate styles, often modeled as
animals, serpents, or plants. This pair,
produced by an unidentified silversmith
working in Zwolle, are in the shape of
scrolled branches decorated with leaves
and fruit.

Nieuwenhuys Wall Sconces
c.1760

These sconces take the form of pendants, each being the exact reverse of the other as shown in the position of the branches. With their asymmetrical design and floral motifs they typify the Louis XV style and were made at Amsterdam by Harmanus Nieuwenhuys (c.1711–63). The back-plates were replaced in 1841 by a pair made by T.G. Bentvelt of Amsterdam.

At A Glance

Date: c.1760
Origin: Holland
Brief description: A pair of two-light wall sconces by Harmanus Nieuwenhuys (1760) with back plates by T.G. Bentvelt, Amsterdam, (1841).

Dominique Wall Sconces
c.1925

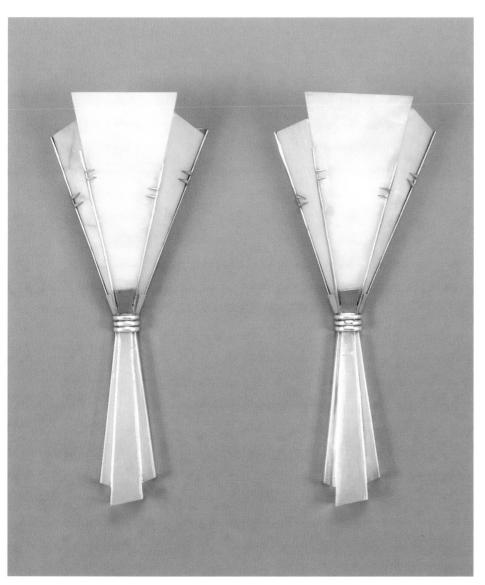

At A Glance

Date: c.1925
Origin: France
Brief description: A pair of silvered bronze wall sconces with alabaster shades made by Dominique, Paris.

This unusual pair of wall sconces has alabaster shades and was designed in the angular, geometric style then coming into fashion. Today this style is generally known as Art Deco, an abbreviation of the Exposition des Arts Décoratifs held in 1924 in Paris, which revolutionized the applied and decorative arts for the ensuing generation.

Danish Candlesticks
post 1945

Each candlestick has a stepped circular base, the long urn form socket emerging from four curling broad stylized leaves. They were designed for Georg Jensen by Harald Nielsen, arguably second only to Johan Rohde among the team of innovative designers who worked for this company in the interwar years.

At A Glance

Date: Post 1945
Origin: Denmark
Brief description: A pair of candlesticks designed by Harald Nielsen in 1930 and executed by Georg Jensen Silversmithy, post 1945.

Five-branch Candelabrum
1945–51

At A Glance

Date: 1945–51
Origin: Denmark
Brief description: A five-branch candelabrum designed by Johan Rohde and made by Georg Jensen.

The gently domed cylindrical base supports a reeded stem on scroll feet, surmounted by the five branches with a central spiral knop and a double dolphin finial. It is designed by Johan Rohde (1856–1935), the painter and designer who collaborated closely with Georg Jensen to revolutionize silver in Scandinavia. This fruitful partnership endured until their deaths, within months of each other in 1935.

Candelabra, Cruet Set, and Dishes
late 19th century

Each pair has knopped stems, scrolled branches, and foliate bobeche, in the style associated with the reign of King George II (1727–60) but still immensely popular today. They are pictured here along with a cruet set and three covered serving dishes all in the same style. They were manufactured by the Gorham Company which produced a considerable quantity of both silver and electroplated hollowwares and candlesticks, especially between about 1887 and the end of the century.

At A Glance

Date: Late 19th century
Origin: USA
Brief description:
  Three-light candelabra, cruet set, and three covered serving dishes all in the style of George II period.

Silver-gilt Group of Figures
late 17th century

At A Glance

Date: Late 17th century.
Origin: Germany/Italy
Brief description: A silver-gilt group of figures depicting the Flagellation.

The figure of Christ is integral to the semi-circular base with a circular well behind flanked by two figures with arms raised.

One of the fine arts revived in the Renaissance period was the modeling and casting of figurines emulating classical models from the sculpture of Greece and Rome. Although bronze was the preferred medium for this work, especially in the larger statuary, many fine pieces were executed in silver, either as individual ornaments or as table centerpieces. This group bears neither the signature of the modeler nor the mark of the founder, but stylistically it is typical of the work of the silversmiths of northern Italy from the late 15th century onward, but in its finish it was more probably manufactured in southern Germany about two centuries later.

Charles II Toilet Service
1680

At A Glance

Date: 1680
Origin: England
Brief description:
 A Charles II twelve-piece toilet service including a large comb-box, two pairs of boxes and covers, a pin-cushion, a pair of pomade pots, a pair of waiters, and a mirror by Jacob Bodendick.

The large octagonal comb-box has a hinged lid decorated with a noble European scene, while the sides are covered by a frieze of birds and foliage. The pair of small octagonal boxes are flat-chased with genre subjects, and the pair of even smaller octagonal boxes are decorated with seated figures, birds, and foliage. To complete the set there is an octagonal pin-cushion, a pair of octagonal baluster pomade-pots, a pair of waiters, and a silver-mounted mirror. This service was made by the Dutch-born London silversmith Jacob Bodendick, and decorated in a more restrained manner than most of his usual wares.

German Pomander
17th century

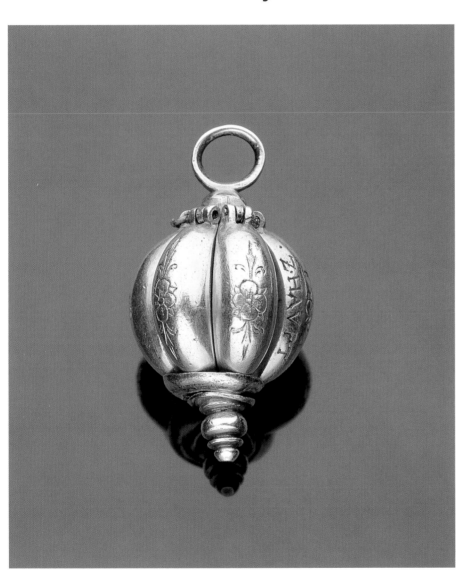

At A Glance

Date: 17th century
Origin: Germany
Brief description: A silver-gilt pomander in the shape of a melon divided into six compartments each engraved with the name of a spice.

Pomander (a corruption of the French Pomme d'Ambre *(apple of amber) were tiny containers filled with spices or perfumes, including amber, usually suspended by a chain round the neck or attached to a chatelaine. In an age when unsanitary conditions prevailed and people seldom bathed, it was useful to take a sniff at the pomander to cover unpleasant smells. This example is shaped like a melon divided into six compartments held together by a baluster screw finial. Each segment has a lid engraved with a spray of flowers and engraved with the name of a spice or perfume.*

A Selection of Pomanders
17th/18th century

At A Glance

Date: 17th/18th century
Origin: Germany
Brief description:
A selection of seven silver pomanders illustrating various shapes and forms.

Pomanders are generally associated with the 17th and 18th centuries, and here is a typical selection from that period comprising: (clockwise from left) a German small silver bottle (early 18th century); a German pomander in the form of a vase (early 18th century); a similar pomander but taller (early 18th century); a pomander with eight hinged segments engraved with the names of spices (17th century); a spherical pomander with six hinged segments engraved with figures and flowers (early 17th century); a pomander with with eight compartments (c.1700); and a small pomander chased as a pineapple with six hinged segments (early 17th century).

William III Casters
1694

A caster is an upright container with a perforated lid designed for sprinkling sugar, pepper, or spices. The earliest examples were generally made of pewter but by the 16th century were also fashioned in silver. Each of these casters has a fluted spreading foot, the body applied with a reeded band, and the partly fluted, pierced, domed covers have bayonet fittings and baluster finials.

At A Glance

Date: 1694
Origin: England
Brief description: A set of three William III cylindrical casters with the maker's mark of "IC."

George III Irish Freedom Caskets
1767–1805

At A Glance

Date: 1767–1805.
Origin: Ireland
Brief description: A group of
  freedom caskets, one in gold
  (top) and the rest in silver. All
  have various versions of the
  civic arms of Cork on the lid
  and the marks of local goldsmiths, such as Carden Terry
  and Jane Williams, Samuel
  Reilly or John Irish.

*Such boxes, designed to contain
the burgess ticket conferring the
freedom of a borough or city,
were usually individually
produced and are often regarded
as masterpieces of craftsmanship.
Their personal association with
the worthy, great, and good gives
them added interest.*

English Buckles
early 19th century

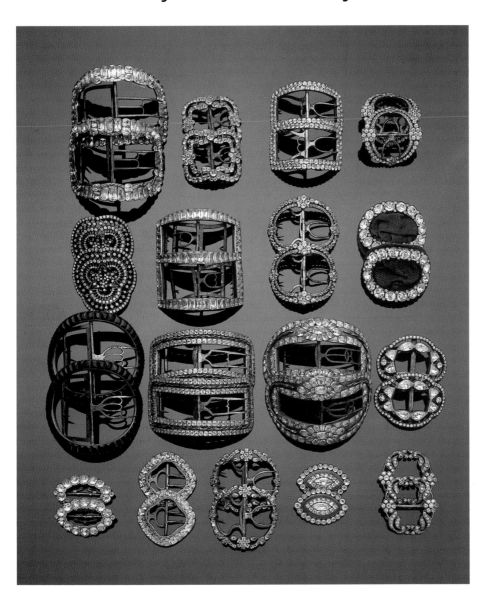

At A Glance

Date: Early 19th century
Origin: England
Brief description: Pairs of metal and paste-set shoe buckles, brooches, and a belt buckle.

Shoe-buckles came into fashion after 1660 when they superseded shoe strings, and continued until about 1800 when straps and laces came back into vogue. Thereafter shoe-buckles continued fitfully on ladies' shoes and Highland brogues, for which reason a high proportion of 19th-century silver buckles will be found with Scottish hallmarks. The vast majority belong to the 18th century, though they are seldom hallmarked before 1790 or bear the maker's mark.

English Vinaigrettes
late 18th/early 19th century

At A Glance

Date: Late 18th/early 19th century.
Origin: England
Brief description: A group of vinaigrettes showing landmarks, scenery, and well-known contemporary personalities.

Vinaigrettes were small silver boxes, devised to hold small sponges soaked in vinegar and aromatic spices as an antidote to contagious diseases and pestilence. They became popular in the 1780s and continued until about 1860 when they were replaced by the double-ended scent bottle. They can be identified by their heavily gilded interiors (to prevent corrosion from the vinegar) and the presence of a perforated inner lid. Their chief interest lies in the pictorial treatment of the outer cover, with landmarks, scenery, and portraits of contemporary celebrities.

Scottish Horn Snuff Mulls
late 18th/early 19th century

At A Glance

Date: Late 18th/early 19th century.
Origin: Scotland
Brief description: A group of 11 silver-mounted, horn, snuff mulls, two inset with cairngorms, mostly inscribed with monograms or inscriptions (two bear dates 1783 and 1855).

The snuff mull is one of the few items of small silver that are peculiarly Scottish (the quaich or whisky cup is another). The basis for the mull was a ram's horn, cut down to the required length near the tip and carefully hollowed out and smoothed. A highly decorative silver rim was fitted with a hinged lid which was usually inscribed with the name or monogram of the owner. In some cases, however, the lids were inset with cairngorms (literally "green stone" in Gaelic, but actually a yellowish-brown quartz found in the Cairngorm Mountains).

Scottish Snuff Mulls and Quaich
1880–1921

One of the silver-mounted snuff mulls has a domed tight-fitting lid embossed with a thistle, the national flower of Scotland, while the other has its lid attached to the horn by a small silver chain. The quaich (from the Gaelic *cuach, a bird's nest*) was a shallow cup with flat handles on opposite sides. The earliest examples, dating from the Middle Ages, were made of wooden staves, often with alternating light and dark woods, but later turned wood and then horn were preferred. By the 18th century, however, silver was the most fashionable medium. They may be found in various sizes and latterly they have been a popular subject for presentation. This highly decorated ornamented example is inscribed "To Lady Irene Corona, 14 July 1921."

At A Glance

Date: 1880–1921
Origin: Scotland
Brief description: Two snuff mulls, one embossed with a thistle, the other with its lid attached by a small silver chain, and a quaich (c.1900) with thistle-shaped handles.

Hutton Silver Casket
1902

Made by William Hutton & Sons of London, this silver box is a fine example of the turn-of-the-century fashion for combining silver with base metals and gems. William Hutton (1774–1842) founded the company in 1800 at Birmingham but later moved the bulk of production to Sheffield. At the beginning of the 20th century Hutton was the largest producer of Art Nouveau silver and electroplate in England.

At A Glance

Date: 1902
Origin: England
Brief description: A decorated silver casket with a hinged cover inset with a high relief panel in mother-of-pearl, pewter, enamel, and copper, showing a lakeside scene applied with scrolling panels set with moonstones.

Cloisonné Cigarette Box
1930

Special cases for carrying cigarettes evolved out of the leather containers for cigars which first became popular in the mid 19th century. After the American Civil War, when cigarettes overtook cigars, special slim cases of papier mâché became popular but after 1900 all-metal cases became fashionable. The silver cigarette case rivaled the snuff-box of an earlier generation as an object of vertu on which cloisonné enameling, filigree work, guilloché engraving and other decorative techniques could be lavished. This example by Bernard Instone bears the Birmingham hallmark of 1930.

At A Glance

Date: 1930
Origin: England
Brief description:
  An enameled silver cigarette case by Bernard Instone.

English Fox-mask Stirrup Cups
1960s

Small drinking cups were developed in the 18th century for the express purpose of giving the riders at the hunt a shot of fortifying spirits on a cold winter's morning before setting off in pursuit of the fox. They were handed up to the rider in the saddle and for that reason required neither a handle nor a foot. Apart from the lack of these features, they are usually identifiable by their distinctive shape in the form of an animal's head—usually a fox. Early examples were made of glass or ceramics but from the early 19th century onward they were generally in silver. The two examples were made in the 1960s but the style has remained virtually unchanged since 1800.

At A Glance

Date: 1960s
Origin: England
Brief description: Two fox-mask stirrup cups with the maker's mark of Wakeley and Wheeler, retailed by Bulgari.

Modern Bowl and Tazza
1988–89

*Here are two splendid examples of modern silver destined to become
the antiques of the future. The parcel-gilt bowl of hemispherical form
has been cast with running foliate decoration by Michael Lloyd, with
the Britannia silver mark and London hallmarks of 1988, while the
silver and slate tazza was crafted by Howard Fenn of London in 1989.*

At A Glance

Date: 1988–89
Origin: England
Brief description: A parcel-gilt bowl cast
with running foliate decoration, stamped
"M.K.L.," and a tazza with a silver bowl
on a polished rectangular slate column,
stamped "HF."

Austrian Desk Set
late 19th century

At A Glance

Date: Late 19th century.
Origin: Austria
Brief description: A silver-gilt and gem-set desk set comprising: a large paper knife, a smaller paper knife, a penknife, and a hand seal.

Writing sets developed from the mid 17th century when standishes with ink pots, pounce pots, pen holders, and other accessories were produced in pewter and later silver. In the 18th century, probably with the growth in popularity of the Grand Tour, traveling sets were devised. Shagreen or leather covered boxes were designed to hold one or more small vessels with tight-fitting lids for ink as well as penholders, seals, and paper knives. This set has a large paper knife with a scimitar blade, a smaller paper knife, a penknife (for cutting quills), and a hand seal, each enameled in white, blue, and green and inset with cabochons. The knives have a filigree baluster finial while the pen has a female mask finial.

Ashtray, Tea Caddy, and Tea Infuser
c.1924

At A Glance

Date: c.1924
Origin: Germany
Brief description:
Ashtray and tea caddy made at the Bauhaus metal workshop, and tea infuser designed in cooperation with Willhelm Wagenfield.

Bauhaus was a school of design that was established in the Weimar in 1919 by Walter Gropius and moved to Dessau in 1926. It was closed in 1933 as a result of Nazi hostility. This ashtray, tea caddy, and tea infuser characterize the Bauhaus esthetic by their emphasis on functional design.

Silver-mounted, Marble Mantel-clock
c.1890

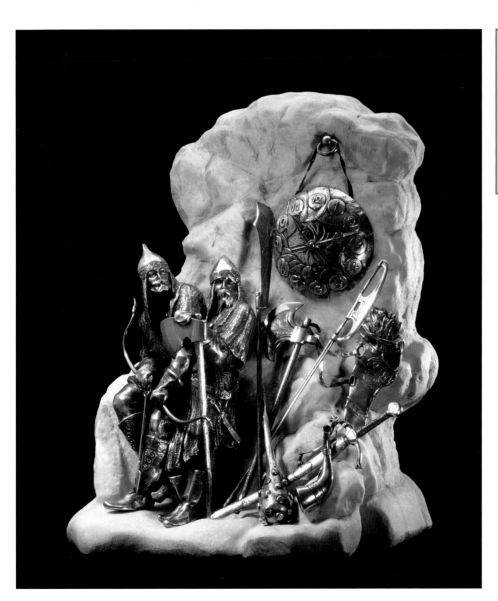

At A Glance

Date: c.1890
Origin: Russia
Brief description: A large silver-mounted, marble mantel-clock with the maker's mark of Pavel Ovchinnikov.

This is a pure example of the Pan-Slavic style which developed among Russian silversmiths in Moscow towards the end of the 19th century. The main feature consists of a pair of realistically cast, carved and chased bearded bogatyrs holding a bow and a large axe among their weaponry and standing against a marble block with a small clock decorated in the Pan-Slavic style. The expression of the bogatyrs is very reminiscent of those in the paintings of Victor Vasnetsov. The silver bears the marks of Pavel Ovchinnikov.